To
Raghav
&
all other batty virtuosos

Contents

Author's Note

This book was not supposed to happen. It did because one night, as I sat in the balcony of my 20th-floor flat in Bengaluru, looking at the city lights, an asteroid-sized idea hit me square in the face. I tumbled, scrambled up and reached for a notebook to jot it all down. That night, I sat with Batty and Foxy and mulled over how scientists invented and discovered crazy things like mind readers and invisible frogs. We wanted to know what made genius brains tick. Why did scientists become, umm, scientists and invent things? What made them spend decades of their lives building a chip with grains of sand or peering at an invisible organism through a microscope? Did they wear lab coats or sanitize their tongues? Did they run out of their showers shouting 'Eureka, Eureka!'?

Our trio decided we would develop a book about the weird, mindboggling things that geniuses spent decades inventing or discovering. 'This is perfect! It'll be my bestselling book,' I exclaimed.

'*Meowr*. Nope. It has no mice,' stated Batty.

'You can't even pronounce or spell the word "ophthalmologist". How will you write on science?' commented Foxy, adjusting her glasses.

My enthusiasm ignored their wise cynicism. I shot out a hopeful email to my marvellous editor, Nimmy Chacko, at Hachette India. Much to my elation (punctuated with Batty's grumble and Foxy's snort), she raved about it. It was on!

After the initial glee came the hard work. When I went looking for masterminds of science in India, I found so many that I was overwhelmed. India's academic institutions, organizations, laboratories and campuses were brimming with passionate, talented people developing incredible, crazy stuff. They spent their lives researching ideas, organisms and concepts I could not even understand ('I told you so,' sniffed Foxy). How could I select a few of these to tell the story of Indian science? ('How can you choose between a brown mouse and a white one?' exclaimed Batty).

As I sat drowning in indecision, Batty hit me on the head and insisted I write about her lifelong passion for genetically modified rodents. 'Nothing else is important,' she declared.

'It needs to be factually correct,' warned Foxy. 'Please refrain from talking about binary nucleocatalyst interstellar space–time craft without explaining what the machine does.' A healthy argument ensued, shaking me out of the rut.

Amongst us, we decided upon the inventions and discoveries that twisted our toes and made us agog with wonder. We found scientists who invented electronic dogs, machines that annoyed plants, rockets to poke Martians and discovered sentimental nerves, cancer-smashing proteins and frogs that were millions of years old. In case some of the peering adults behind your shoulders feel we missed important Indian scientists or your aunt's research, pen down your criticisms and write to Batty or Foxy. They have graciously agreed to tackle any fan mail that comes my way. (I take sole responsibility for every Horrible Haiku.)

Before I leave you to discover the hidden wonders in this book, I would like to thank a few elves who scrambled behind the scenes to get this scientific feat together. There is Nimmy, of course, and the editorial and marketing team at Hachette India, which actively hatched the plot. A special thanks goes to Rajita Gadagkar for her magical ability to chop sentences and save us pages, Utpal Chattopadhyay who aided Foxy in making sure I get facts right, and Sharanya Kunnath for the covers and drawing Batty's likeness and other things. Also to my silently suffering husband Ashwani, who calmly weathered the storm that was me, and all the other invisible creatures we share our lives with. And that... *Thunk!* Oww!

Do not forget the most important contribution of Batty and her rightful passion for rodent-destruction mechanisms and Foxy who obsesses over yawn-inducing facts. I leave you all, my dear loony geniuses, in their able paws and jaws, to keep digging, prying and finding new possibilities in our world.

Keep scouting the skies!

Shweta Taneja
Zapping at www.shwetawrites.com

1

A Sixty-Million-Year-Old Frog

The frog had pale blue dots on its glistening brown body. When the light shone on it, the dots glittered. Like stars. When you turned the frog over, it had a bright orange underbelly, like a sunrise. The mysterious creature was tiny, the size of a thumbnail. It lay hidden under a dried leaf in the thick canopy of a tree. Vijay and his team would have missed it completely, had he not been an expert on frogs.

SP Vijayakumar, or Vijay as his friends called him, was a doctoral researcher at the Indian Institute of Science (IISc) in Bengaluru and an ecologist. He'd encountered the frog on one of his nightly hikes through the dense forests of the Western Ghats. The Ghats, a green, mist-soaked mountain range in the south of India was a biodiversity hotspot*. Also called

*The Western Ghats in India is one of just 36 biodiversity hotspots around the world. A biodiversity hotspot is a region that has a huge variety

the Sahyadri, the thick wilderness hid more than 250 species of amphibians[†] – the type of creatures that Vijay specialized in researching.

When the leaf in the woods rustled slightly, Vijay had crouched on the forest bed to investigate.

'Is that a *Nyctibatrachus*?' asked his colleagues, Saunak and Mrugank, as they inspected the frog, an expert at hiding. *Nyctibatrachus* was a group of night frogs commonly found in the Western Ghats.

'It does look like one, but the starry patterns are different. And here, look...' Vijay picked up the frog in the palm of his hand, upturning it carefully, '...the toe pads are different from *Nyctibatrachus*. Or any other frog we've seen!'

On their nocturnal rambles, Vijay and his team listened for, photographed and collected rare specimens of frogs, lizards and snakes that hopped on and slithered across the dark forest floor. It was their job to study these amphibians and reptiles. They were all part of Kartik Shanker's laboratory at the Centre for Ecological Sciences (CES) at IISc. Kartik was their professor and a fellow ecologist.

---

of plants, birds, mammals, reptiles and amphibian species. These sites support nearly 60 per cent of the world's species. Understanding how these regions work and how to save them is very important. The Western Ghats is home to at least 84 amphibian species, 16 bird species, seven mammal species and 1,600 flowering plants that are not found anywhere else in the world.

[†]Amphibians are animals that live partly on land and partly in water. Examples include frogs, toads, salamanders, newts and caecilians (limbless creatures that look like worms or snakes).

HORRIBLE HAIKU

Dark, aged forest
An eager ecologist
Pounces on
A wrinkled frog

The team had been surveying the Ghats for several years now, combing through them day and night. The survey, which began sometime in 2010, was intense.

The aim was simple – to collect samples of various species of amphibians and reptiles and bring them back to the CES lab*. At the lab, the samples or 'specimens' (as scientists call them) would be more closely examined, their physical traits listed. Eventually, the group would also sequence[†] the genes of all the specimens collected. This would help them understand the evolutionary relationships[§] between various species.

That particular night had been frustrating for Vijay and his team. They had trudged through the cold – sampling, recording, taking photos and writing notes – while being bitten by mosquitoes and sucked

*Ecologists take permission from forest officials to collect a few specimens of the species they want to research. After photographing them and collecting them as samples, the specimens are taken back to the lab. Here they are euthanized following scientific protocols. They are then treated with chemicals to preserve them for further study and stored in the lab. Kartik's lab has hundreds of different amphibians collected from the Western Ghats, which his students study.

[†]A sequencing method is a scientific process to reveal genetic information that is carried in the particular DNA of a creature.

[§]Evolutionary relationships is a scientific term used to describe genetic similarities or variations between different species.

on by leeches. Vijay was tired and wanted to go back to his field station (the base they had set up near the forest). But he was excited about the new discovery.

'Let's take a sample,' suggested one of his colleagues. Vijay agreed, in a hurry to get some sleep. They picked up the frog and put it in their sample bag along with dozens of other specimens. Later, they found out that they had picked up 15 to 20 different types of frogs that night. But none was as remarkable as the one with stars on its back.

After he reached the CES lab, Vijay passed on the sample of the elusive frog from the Ghats to Varun Torsekar, another student in Kartik Shanker's laboratory, who specialized in studying night frogs.

Their professor Kartik was an evolutionary biologist. His job was to figure out how different species of animals, say in Africa and India, were related to each other. To do this, his team at the CES lab studied their DNA and built evolutionary trees which mapped the relationships between species.

Kartik encouraged his students to study a variety of frogs, lizards, snakes and even marine fauna. But a single species, even if it was a new one, was not that important to their research in evolutionary biology. Since Varun could not find an immediate connection between the starry frog and other night frogs, they tagged it, added it to their collection and put it away.

HOW ECOLOGISTS SAVE THE FORESTS

When ecologists like Vijay and Kartik study how frogs are related to each other, how does it help a frog living in the middle of a forest in the Western Ghats?

Scientists who work with wildlife can be ecologists, biologists or conservationists. They want to know why natural spaces like forests are important for both humans and other species. They gather information, do field studies, and collect data on various plants and animals and their habitats.

With this data, they understand different things about the climate and Earth. Like what the effects of climate change are, where particular species are found or why some animal populations are dwindling worldwide. Scientists show these findings to governments and work with society so they can protect wildlife and forests.

In the 1980s, Madhav Gadgil, the scientist who started the CES at IISc, helped to establish the Nilgiri Biosphere Reserve, the first one

in the country. In 2011, he submitted a report that convinced the government to identify the Western Ghats as an 'Ecologically Sensitive Area' (ESA). This meant that people would need permission from the government to build roads, cut trees or do farming there.

In another instance, scientists worked with the Bugun tribe in Arunachal Pradesh to protect the Bugun liocichla, a critically endangered bird species.

There are conservation projects that are aimed at protecting and securing wildlife corridors in the country, which enable free movement of animals from one forest to another.

Despite these advances, a lot of questions about the natural world remain unanswered. For instance, why have deciduous forests become drier? Are forest fires burning at higher temperatures because there is not enough moisture in the soil? How does climate change affect the migration of birds, and flowering and fruiting? Will we face more deadly viruses if forests are cut down?

India needs more ecologists, biologists, botanists, ornithologists and zoologists to find answers to these pressing issues so that we can save our forests. What kind of ecological problems do you observe around you? Can they be solved by a scientist? List five of these problems and their possible solutions.

Vijay went back to the Western Ghats several times in the following years. He found 20 new types of bush frogs (a species prevalent in the Western Ghats), of which nine were eventually found to be new species previously unknown to scientists. All this while, the starry frog lay forgotten in a drawer in the CES lab.

A few years later, Kartik was on a field trip with a student, Navendu Page, when the starry frog came up in conversation.

'Remember the frog...the one that Vijay found?' Navendu said. 'He mentioned that it might be an entirely new genus.'

Discovering new species was important, but not the focus of evolutionary biologists. However, finding an entirely new genus was a great discovery, though tough to prove! This meant that the starry frog's DNA could tell them a lot about frog evolution and migration from millions of years ago.

Kartik rushed back from the field to the lab and called a meeting with Vijay and Varun. Vijay took the forgotten frog out of the drawer and the three scientists inspected it closely once again. They realized how different it was from any other frog they had seen, with its star-shaped dots and orange belly. Being scientists, they had to be sure that the frog was a unique find – a new genus. This meant that they had to make a list of not just its external features, bone structure and behaviour, but also of its genetics.

Batty cat cracks

What's in a genus? A mouse of any family will be yummy to Batty.

'Let's get other scientists involved,' said Kartik, realizing that they were onto something big.

To describe the species form, Kartik, Vijay and Varun brought in KP Dinesh, a scientist at the Zoological Survey of India (ZSI) in Pune. He had been a postdoctoral researcher in Kartik's lab and was interested in frogs too.

Dinesh went back to the spot that Vijay had visited in the Western Ghats seven years ago to find the starry frog and observe it in its habitat. He collected all the additional data required for the description of the starry frog. The frog did not match any of the ones listed in their catalogue. It was definitely a new species. But to figure out if it was a new genus or sub-family, they had to dig through all the databases – in the whole world!

Kartik and his team contacted Alex Pyron, a professor at George Washington University in the USA. He had compiled the genetic data of over 4,000 amphibians from every part of the world. Working their way through it, the researchers could map how the new species was related to other frog species. Kartik also sent a CT scan* of the frog's skeleton to US-based scientists David Blackburn and Edward Stanley at the Florida Museum. They compared the starry frog's bone structure to other frog species from the Western Ghats.

Both teams got back with the same result. The starry frog was entirely different from any frog that had been described before. They found that its closest relatives were the family of *Nyctibatrachidae*, a group of over 30 species native to India and Sri Lanka.

Further analysis revealed something truly amazing. The sub-family of the frog had diversified or branched off around 60 to 70 million years ago, and had stayed isolated since then. This meant that it was not only a new genus, but it was also the descendant of an ancient lineage of frogs at least 60 million years old! 'This frog has had no sister species for tens of millions of years!' exclaimed Vijay.

Kartik's team of ecologists named the starry frog *Astrobatrachus kurichiyana*. 'Astro' (Greek for star) was for its constellation-like markings, 'batrachus' stood for frog and 'kurichiyana' was derived from the Kurichiyar tribe who live in the hills where the frog has made its home.

*A medical imaging technology, this scan allows you to see inside an object without cutting it open.

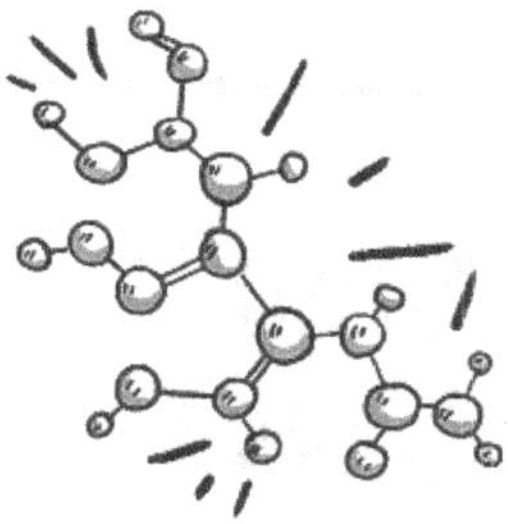

SCIENCE SPEAK

THE MAGIC OF TEAMWORK

Kartik and his team could have managed to prove that the starry frog was a new genus on their own. They could have published the results without the skeletal data and even built a genetic tree by themselves. But it would have taken them a lot longer to get the results.

Scientists collaborate with their peers in other countries either because they want to or because the nature of their research demands it. Kartik liked to make new connections and collaborate scientifically. It added to the fun of scientific discovery!

Connecting with scientists around the world and reading their research is an important part of scientific work. Collaborating is the best way to achieve more, create change and help humankind.

Finally, in 2019, almost a decade after Vijay first found it, they published a paper on their findings in a science journal.

As you read this, Kartik, Vijay and the team at CES continue their quest to find rare and marvellous frogs, snakes and lizards in the Western Ghats.

I spy a scientist who works on Valparai's forest restoration. Can you name that person?

____

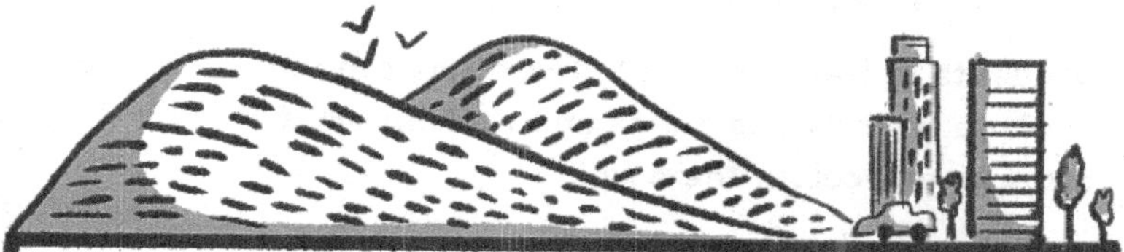

Time for a Sound Check!

Take a walk outside your home or open your window. Sit and listen. How many different animal sounds do you hear? If you live in a city you may hear cats, dogs, squirrels, bees, flies, mosquitoes and several different birds. If you live in the countryside you will probably hear more. List out the sounds here:

Colour These Fantastic Frogs

Students at Kartik's lab at IISc study the following frogs. Look up their names online and find out what colours they are. Can you colour them right?

1. Malabar gliding frog
Rhacophorus malabaricus
2. Chalazodes bush frog
Raorchestes chalazodes
3. Starry dwarf frog
Astrobatrachus kurichiyana
4. Torrent frog
Micrixalus sp.
5. Night frog
Nyctibatrachus sp.

Art credit: Achyuthan Srikanthan

2

A New Way to Scatter Light

It was a bright summer's day in the sleepy town of Thiruvanaikkaval in Kerala. Little Chandrasekhara Venkata Raman lay in the garden staring up at the sky.

'Stop daydreaming, Raman, and pass me the ball!' his brother yelled.

Raman looked up at his brother and rolled towards the ball, which lay a few feet away from him. He picked it up, looked back up at the sky and stopped midway.

'Raman!'

But the boy didn't hear his brother call. He dropped the ball and dashed into the house, heading straight to the living room where his mother, Parvathi Ammal, sat.

'Amma, Amma! Why is the colour of the sky blue?'

'Because of the sun,' she replied, used to her ever-inquisitive son's constant questions.

Raman would come up to her with a new question every day, wanting to know why things were the way they were, and how everything worked. He went back into the garden and stared up at the sky again. Amma's answer made no sense to him. The sun's rays were white, he thought, so what made the sky *blue*?

In the evening, his father, a schoolteacher, got home from work and started tuning his violin. As Raman watched him, another question popped into his head. He stood close to his father, his nose two inches away from the violin's strings.

'What are you doing?' asked his father, amused.

'Why does the violin sound different from the veena?' Raman asked.

'Parvathi,' his father called out, 'your son has yet another question!'

This was the 1890s – more than 120 years ago – when being curious was a problem. Books were not easily available, and there was no Internet, of course. So you couldn't just voice search the answers to the things you wanted to know. Raman's teachers would break into a sweat or look the other way when they saw the young boy walking towards them with a new doubt brewing in his head.

Raman (and his parents) got some respite in 1904, when he received a scholarship to study at the Presidency College in Madras (now called Chennai). There, the 16-year-old had access to a scientific laboratory for the first time. One day he noticed a prism lying on a table and picked it up, observing how the light entered from one side and escaped in a flurry of colours. He let out a whoop of joy! He finally had a chance to figure out the answers to the questions burning inside him.

SCIENCE SPEAK

VIOLIN VERSUS VEENA

Why does a violin sound different from Indian stringed instruments? The question that had baffled Raman as a child led him to study the construction of the veena and tanpura. He found out that Indian instruments were designed to mimic the sounds of a human voice. This made them sound different from Western instruments.

The first pressing issue he decided to address was to do with light. He would sit for hours with the prism, observing how light refracted into a rainbow of colours. While measuring the angle of a prism using a spectrometer*, Raman observed some diffraction

*A spectrometer is a scientific instrument used to separate and measure light, its wavelength, frequency and intensity.

bands*. A brilliant and enthusiastic student, he investigated them and published his first paper in 1906.

At the age of 18, Raman finished his studies, got married and started working as a civil servant in Kolkata. It was a good, steady job. But his favourite scientific conundrums continued to bother him. Every day, as he headed to work by tram, he would look up and wonder why the sky was such a vivid blue.

One day, on his way to work, he spotted a broken sign with the name 'The Indian Association for the Cultivation of Science' on Bowbazaar Street. He scrambled out of the tram and sprinted towards the sign. He knocked on the door of the building and met the secretary of the association, Amrita Lal Sircar.

'I want to do research here,' said Raman, panting.

Amrita Lal grinned and welcomed him inside. He had been looking for a scientist to lead the association.

The 1900s were a fascinating time to study physics. Scientists around the world were doing a whole bunch of revolutionary experiments. Radiation, X-rays and electrons had recently been discovered. Iconic physicist Albert Einstein was in the process of developing his special and general theory of relativity, which would go on to become the basis of modern physics and change the world. Around the turn of the century, JJ Thompson and E. Rutherford had developed the basic ideas of what atoms were made of, and Max Planck had

*When a beam of light is partly blocked by an obstacle, the light goes around the obstacle and forms light and dark bands along the edge of the shadows. This effect is called diffraction.

put forth revolutionary ideas about the energy of light and quantum physics, which changed the way scientists looked at the world around them.

Inventors were creating all kinds of remarkable equipment to observe what happened at this invisible, atomic level.

Even Raman's question about the colour of the sky was answered by a phenomenon called light scattering. Lord Rayleigh discovered that the sky was blue because it was blue light from the spectrum that was thrown sideways when sunlight passed through the air. If the red light of the spectrum had been thrown sideways, our sky would have looked dark ruby!

This increased Raman's interest in researching light, its properties and how it scattered. Along with Ashutosh Dey, another scientist at the association, he started working on discovering more about light. As they didn't have a lot of money for their research, they had to make do with scientific instruments put together from everyday things found in local shops. The two scientists picked up chains and hubs from old cycles and disused optical benches. Out of motley objects, they fashioned an apparatus which had a mirror for deflecting sunlight, a condensing lens, a pair of complimentary glass filters, a flask containing benzene and a pocket spectroscope to scatter* white light. Their fully equipped laboratory was now ready for experiments!

*When light passes through one medium – gas, liquid or solid – a part of it is absorbed by particles in this medium. The rest comes out in different directions. This is called scattering of light.

Batty cat cracks

Dr Spectrometer, Batty wants a rat prism. Feed a white rat from one end and give Batty seven rats in the seven colours of the rainbow. *Purr.*

In his new lab, Raman decided to look into the phenomenon that had perplexed him since he was a child – how light fractured and scattered in different directions and colours when it passed through different gases, liquids and some solids. If it passed through a prism, for example, it became a rainbow of colours. In the sky, light from the sun would scatter because of gases like nitrogen and oxygen. In liquids like water, light would scatter and refract in different ways. 'Water has 160 times more scattering power than air,' observed Raman.

Even though his days were long and tiring, Raman loved every minute of it. He would wake up at 5.30 a.m. and head to the association to do his experiments. He would come back home, have breakfast and leave for his office at 9.45 a.m. At 5 p.m., Raman headed straight back to the association and only reached home at 10 p.m.

FOXY FACTS

THE ULTIMATE PHYSICS GLOSSARY

What is refraction? It's the change in the direction of light when it passes through a medium with a different density than the one it has been moving through. For instance, light refracts when it passes through a prism from air, or through water from air.

What is an atom? An atom is the smallest unit of matter. Everything in the universe – solids, liquids, gases and plasma, and our own bodies – is made up of these extremely small units.

What are X-rays? A type of see-through electromagnetic radiation that passes through most solid objects, including our bodies.

What is radiation? It is the transmission of energy in the form of waves or particles through space or through a medium.

What is ultraviolet light? It is a type of radiation that extends from the violet part of the spectrum to the X-ray region. Humans cannot see this radiation. But when it falls on some materials, it may cause them to fluoresce or emit electromagnetic radiation, which is translated as low-energy visible light.

Soon, he started welcoming other students and researchers into the association, people who were equally passionate about research. They began publishing papers and became famous in Kolkata, even starting their own journal dedicated to science.

The vice chancellor of Calcutta University at that time was so impressed by Raman's passion for physics that he offered him a full-time professorship. In 1917, with the money granted by the university, Raman promptly opened another laboratory and invited a number of students to study light with him. Now, he had two places where he could conduct experiments to his heart's content!

A few months later, Raman's university sent him to Europe to meet other scientists and gain experience. While coming back home by ship, he ran an experiment with a prism. 'Even when the reflection of the sky is controlled, the sea remains a deep blue,' he concluded. He wondered if like air, water also scattered light causing the blue waters.

Back in India, Raman hurried to his lab, wanting to research the scattering of light in liquids. He brought out a large bottle of a clear, transparent liquid called toluene and passed a beam of light through it. The liquid turned a brilliant blue. This proved what he had suspected all along: the water in the sea looked blue due to its own light scattering. Next, he added a prism between the source of light and water. He put various filters in the middle to see how the light would refract. He also sent X-rays through liquids and recorded the results.

Without a break Raman immersed himself in new problems. One evening, while he was experimenting in his lab with another scientist, Srinivasa Krishnan, he discovered something peculiar. As light went through different liquids, a part of it scattered in reverse. This behaviour was different from the light scattering that he had observed earlier. It was because of the presence of a trace of *something*.

Ramanathan, one of Raman's students, came across the same *something* when studying the scattering of light in water. At first, both thought it was an impurity in the liquids they were using. So they repeated the process after purifying distilled water further. The effect remained. Ramanathan gave it the name 'weak fluorescence'.

The trio discussed what this new *something* could be. They investigated 60 liquids for light scattering in 1924, and observed that this mysterious phenomenon happened in all of them. However, they couldn't form a theory around it and abandoned their research in 1925.

Like the question of the light scattering in liquids that mystified him, the phenomenon of 'weak fluorescence' gave Raman sleepless nights. One day, he woke up in a flash of inspiration. The *something* that he couldn't pin down was probably not a material, but a completely new kind of radiation emitted by the light itself. He was excited by the idea of residual light waves that hadn't been observed before. A new type of scattering!

EXCUSE ME. WHERE'S YOUR SLIPPER?

Raman was known to be quite forgetful, especially when he was working on a scientific problem, which was on most days. He would often forget to eat food, change his clothes or even sleep!

One day, the absent-minded professor was invited to speak at the Shorthand Writers' Association in Kolkata, where he was the president. As he climbed up the stage, someone pointed at his feet. He looked down and frowned. He was wearing only one sandal! He had forgotten the other at home.

On another day, as he set off for his lab in the morning, he realized he didn't have a shirt or coat on! A few days after, he wore his coat inside out. Another time, while speaking at a convention, he started drinking coffee, tilting the cup near his lips, while continuing to speak. The coffee, meanwhile, spilled over, splashing on his clothes. He didn't notice till someone from the audience alerted him!

Along with his fellow researcher Srinivasa, Raman locked himself up in the lab and conducted a slew of experiments. The first step was to see if all liquids showed this effect. They used a powerful beam of sunlight from a heliostat, an apparatus fitted with a movable mirror to reflect sunlight in a particular direction. This was passed through a blue-violet filter and into the liquid. They examined 80 liquids and found that the same scattering of light happened in all of them. This was a kind of light scattering that hadn't been observed before.

Krishnan and Raman had found a new physical phenomenon, a new way of scattering of light by matter!

Using a spectroscope, they observed that the new type of scattering was clearly marked as a separate dark space. To further investigate it, they set up an impressive glowing contraption called the mercury arc. Raman's favourite instrument to study light, it was made to emit monochromatic (of one colour) light. When a filter was used to cut off all visible light, the spectroscope revealed two sharp lines in the blue-green region.

Finally, they were able to visualize and take pictures of the line spectrum of the new radiation. Raman announced his discovery to the press and the newspaper carried the story the next day with the headline, 'New theory of radiation: Prof Raman's discovery'.

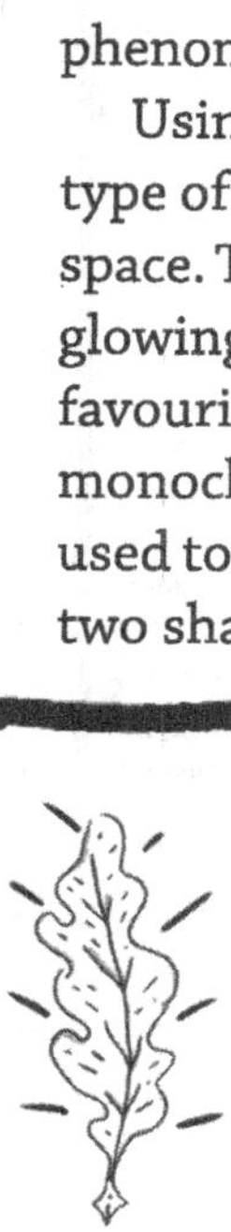

HORRIBLE HAIKU

Light breaks a leg
Rainbow peeks
Out of the
spectrometer

In 1930, Raman was awarded the Nobel Prize for this discovery of the new type of light scattering that now bears his name. On receiving the Nobel Prize, he said, 'I am sad that India does not have a flag of her own.' To honour the physicist, 28 February, the day that 'Raman effect' was discovered, is celebrated as 'Indian Science Day'.

Meow! Batty always knew not wearing boots wins one Nobel Prize.

SCIENCE SPEAK

A TALE OF TWO SCIENCE HEROINES

Kamala Sohonie was determined to become a scientist like her father and her uncle. Unfortunately, in the early 20th century, not many women could become scientists. But Kamala was resolute. After graduating from Bombay University, she applied to study in CV Raman's laboratory in Bangalore in 1933.

The Nobel laureate refused her admission. Women can't do research, he told her. Kamala refused to take no for an answer. She sat outside his office for days to protest his decision. He finally gave in and granted her admission. 'You will work for one year on probation,' he said, sternly.

Kamala squared her shoulders and nodded. Her teacher, Professor Sreenivasayya, was strict and demanding. She worked hard and specialized in biochemistry, researching proteins in milk, pulses and legumes to see how their nutritional value could be improved.

After years of unflinching hard work, she became the first Indian woman to get a Ph.D from Cambridge University in the UK. Her determination also made Raman realize how wrong he was. From then on, women students were welcome in his lab. One of them was Anna Mani.

On Anna's eighth birthday, her father, a civil engineer, offered her diamond earrings as a gift. To everyone's surprise, she said that she wanted books so she could understand how the universe worked.

After graduating, she joined IISc in 1940 and began working with Raman. At that time, the physicist was studying the molecular structure of diamonds and how they vibrated when heat passed through them. Anna recorded and analysed the properties of different diamonds.

After her research, she left for England, where she specialized in designing meteorological instruments. The physicist and meteorologist returned to India after Independence in 1948 and worked on the construction of radiation instrumentation. Her father always joked that Anna Mani's obsession with diamonds started only after she became a scientist!

Sleuth Snoop

I spy another Nobel laureate in this book. Who is that and what did they find?

____

____

A SHINY, SPARKLY OBSESSION

Anyone who knew Raman knew he was obsessed with diamonds. His favourite haunts were jewellery stores and pawn shops in Kolkata, where he would rummage for old pieces that belonged to Indian royalty. He wanted to get his hands on all kinds of diamonds so that he could use them for his light scattering experiments. 'To carry out my work on diamonds, I have to make a collection,' he said to himself.

When he ran out of money, he reached out to his rich friends to borrow their diamonds. Some were obviously hesitant at first. After all, Raman was asking for their most prized possessions.

Raman was still not satisfied. He wanted to procure diamonds in their natural shape, not the ones that were polished or changed in any way. In those days, the best mine for diamonds was in Palam in north India. Raman went there and examined thousands of diamonds in their natural form. He found out that the maharaja of Palam had a garland of 52 large diamonds of 60 or 70

carats each, all in their natural form. Raman's eyes shone. 'The very best diamonds India has ever produced!' he exclaimed. 'Can I have them please?'

The maharaja was surprised at the request but donated the garland for the purpose of scientific research. (This one Raman did return once he was done with his experiments!) Years later, Raman was honoured with a pendant of 63 diamonds by the maharaja of Mysore. He promptly brought the gift back to his lab and studied all the diamonds to observe what happened to them when they were exposed to ultraviolet light.

'Why are you studying these diamonds?' asked a visitor. 'Are you trying to make them in your laboratory?'

'If I do, you could use them as a perfect cooking vessel,' exclaimed Raman. 'You see, if you illuminate a diamond with ultraviolet light, it becomes an excellent electrical conductor.'

By the end of his life, Raman had a collection of over 600 diamonds of different types!

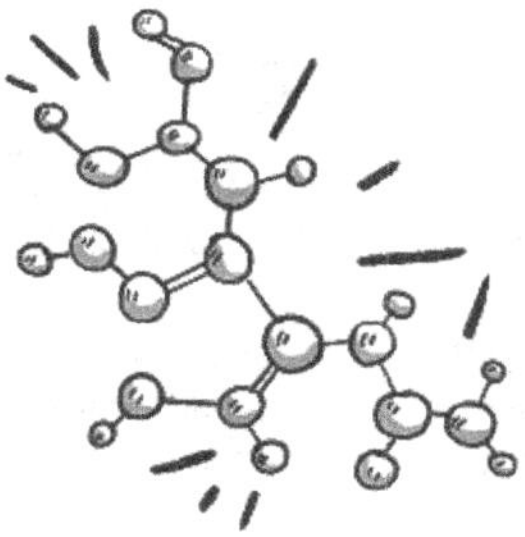

SCIENCE SPEAK

ERRR... WHAT IS THE RAMAN EFFECT?

Light and X-rays are both electromagnetic radiation that interact with matter and molecules. Radiation can be scattered, absorbed or re-emitted, leaving behind the molecule unchanged, energetically excited or decomposed. In the Raman effect, the light gets scattered by the molecule and the molecule is left in an energy state different from its initial stage. Effectively, there is a change in the wavelength of light that occurs when a light beam is deflected by molecules.

The Raman effect has opened new directions in science research – in the study of light spectrums, chemistry and quantum mechanics (a field that describes the physical properties of nature at the level of atoms and subatomic particles). Even a hundred years after Raman and his team found this special spectrum, scientists are still experimenting with this type of scattering.

Make your own Spectroscope

You'll Need:

- Empty paper towel roll
- Scissors
- Old CD
- Pencil
- Small piece of cardboard
- Tape
- Paint

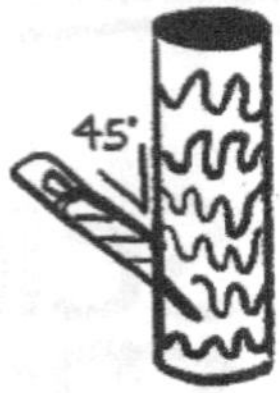

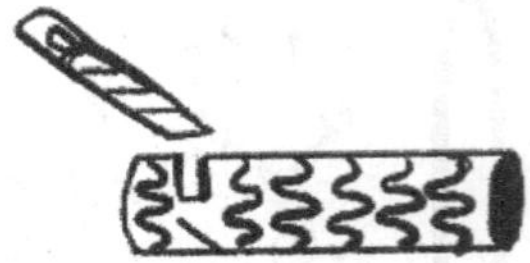

1 If you want to paint the spectroscope, paint the paper towel roll and let it dry.

2 Take the dried roll and use a knife (an adult might need to help you here) to cut a thin slit at a 45° angle towards the bottom of the cardboard tube.

3 Directly across from the slit, make a small peephole.

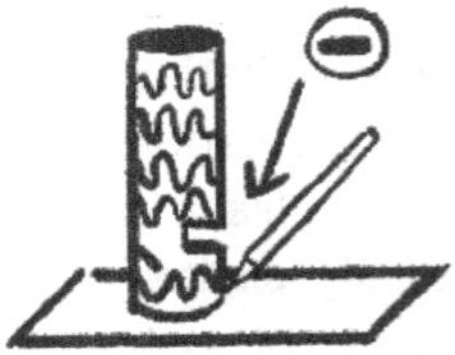

4 Trace one end of your paper towel roll onto a small piece of cardboard. Cut it out into a circle and inside the circle, cut a straight rectangular slit in the centre.

5 Now tape the cardboard circle to the top of your spectroscope.

6 Insert a CD in the 45° angle slit, shiny side facing up.

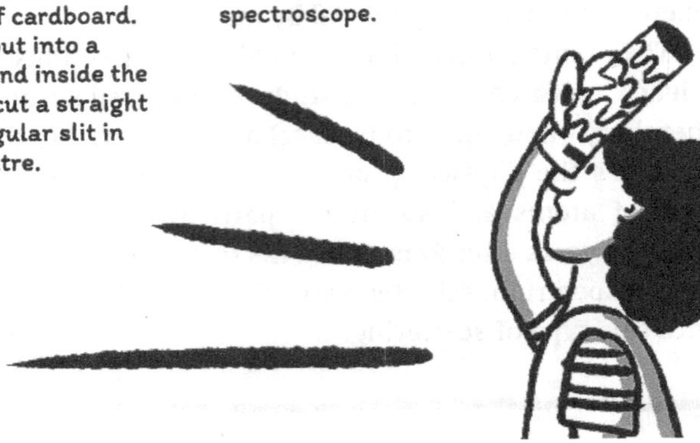

3

A Drug to Reverse Memory Loss

Back in 1983, when Vijayalakshmi Ravindranath saw a section of a brain under a microscope for the first time, she fell in love with it. It was not the ugly brown lump that she had seen in photographs. It was a sophisticated, seamless organ – an intricate web of connections. And what a web it is! A human brain has 86 billion nerve cells called neurons*, billions of nerve fibres (called axons and dendrites) and trillions of connections or synapses between them. There are gazillions of microscopic moving parts, faithfully recording signals from various parts of the body – transferring them, converting them and acting on them. It is a compact universe held in one and a half kilograms of flesh.

Vijayalakshmi, who worked as a postdoctoral researcher at the National Cancer Institute in the USA,

*Neurons are brain cells that communicate with one another through electrical impulses.

was fascinated. She would keep staring at a neuron under the microscope, spellbound. 'This is pure joy,' she told her colleague. 'No two neurons are alike. It is like an organized jigsaw puzzle where each part is unique, but with a purpose.' It was like looking at a very, very advanced computer, the command centre of the human body that controlled everything in it. It was at this exact moment that Vijayalakshmi decided to become a neuroscientist – a scientist who researches the brain.

As a child, Vijayalakshmi wanted to become an engineer, but her parents did not like the idea. So she chose to study chemistry instead. After getting her graduate and postgraduate degrees from Andhra University, she joined a doctoral programme in organic chemistry at IISc in Bengaluru, where she met her future husband. After getting married, Vijayalakshmi moved to Mysore, where she began to do research at the Central Food Technological Institute (CFTI) on a powerful chemical with anti-cancerous properties called curcumin (found in turmeric or haldi).

After getting a Ph.D in biochemistry at IISc, the scientist moved to the USA to do a postdoctoral fellowship at the National Cancer Institute in Bethseda, Maryland. The day she first gazed at a human brain under the microscope at the institute, she was hooked, and she made it the focus of her research.

When Vijayalakshmi returned to India, she joined the National Institute of Mental Health and Neuro-Sciences (NIMHANS) in Bengaluru.

SCIENCE SPEAK

THE NERVE OF IT!

The nervous system is a complex network of nerves and specialized cells called neurons. This network forms the body's electrical wiring. Its job is to receive and transmit the information we take in from the environment. It also regulates the activities of the body, from muscle movement to blood pressure and breathing.

Neuroscience is a field of science that explores the workings of the human brain and the nervous system, combining various fields of science like physiology, anatomy, biology, mathematical modelling and psychology.

At the mental health and neuroscience institute, she saw people with neurodegenerative diseases*, who experienced physical and mental handicaps as their nervous systems – especially the neurons in their brains – wore out or died over time. Patients often lost the ability for movement or forgot things (even the faces and names of loved ones). Within a month of observing these patients, Vijayalakshmi decided that she wanted to help them. Everyone should have a smoothly working, well-oiled, healthy brain even as they age, she thought.

Along with her team of students, she began investigating the neuroscience behind various brain disorders. Vijayalakshmi could be found seated on a bench, hunched over a microscope, observing and noting down stuff for hours on end. She was rewarded with her first breakthrough in 1990. The neuroscientist and her team found that the brain behaved like the liver. It absorbed and metabolized drugs. This had never been observed before!

After 10 years at NIMHANS, Vijayalakshmi, who by now was a well-known neuroscientist, was invited to Delhi to set up the National Brain Research Centre in 1997. She spent the next decade setting up the centre and coordinating efforts in brain research across the Indian scientific community. Her research focused on a brain disorder that affected elderly people: dementia.

*Neurodegenerative diseases are diseases caused when your central nervous system is not working well or your nerve cells are dying. Examples include Alzheimer's, Parkinson's and Huntington's. These diseases have no known cure and cause physical and mental disabilities as nerve cells die or degenerate.

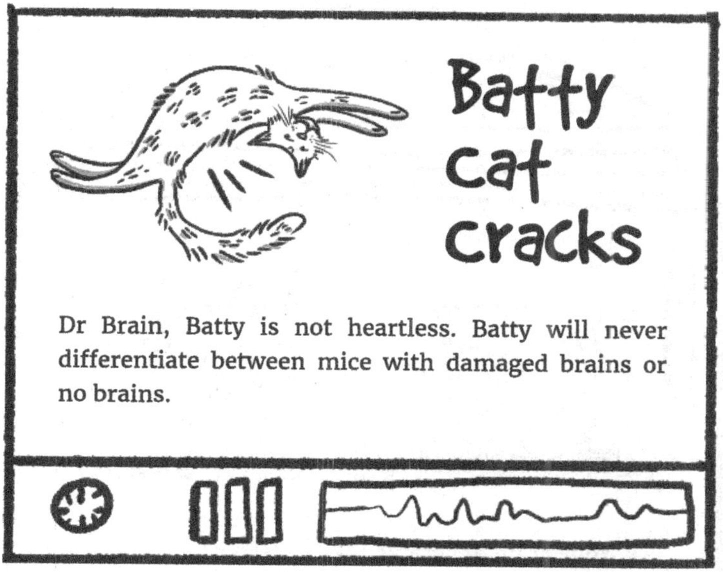

Those with this condition experienced memory loss – they forgot how to speak, perform their daily routines and could not remember who they were and where they lived. Eventually, some of them lost the ability to recognize family and friends.

When Vijayalakshmi was conducting this research, there were no drugs to treat dementia. She collaborated with Ayurveda practitioners to develop one by identifying a plant extract that could possibly be used to reverse the damages of memory loss. The extract was given to laboratory mice.

Four weeks into the study, her student Alok Gupta was examining the brains of the mice. Usually, a dementia-affected brain has a lot of protein deposits.

FOXY FACTS

YOUR NUTTY, COOL BRAIN

→ Your brain generates 12–25 watts of electricity. It's enough to power a low-wattage LED bulb!

→ You don't use most of your brain power. If you did, you could solve mathematical problems quicker than a computer!

→ You can perform brain surgery on a person while they are awake as the brain has no pain receptors and feels no pain.

→ Your brain cannot multitask. What it does is quickly switch back and forth from different tasks.

→ There are 25,00,000 gigabytes of storage space in your brain.

- → If you laid out all of the blood vessels in your brain end-to-end, they would stretch to about 97,000 kilometers. That's about double the Earth's circumference.
- → There are about 100 billion neurons in your brain – about the same number as the stars in the Milky Way.
- → Feeling tired? Yawn more. Yawning cools down the brain. Sleep deprivation raises brain temperature. Now you know what to say the next time your teacher catches you yawning in class!
- → About 73 per cent of your brain is made of water.
- → The brain weighs about 1.5 kilograms. Although it makes up just 2 per cent of the body's weight, it uses around 20 per cent of its energy!

When he observed one particular brain, he saw something unexpected. He pushed back his chair and ran to Vijayalakshmi's office, calling out to her. Seeing his excitement, Vijayalakshmi hurried after him to the lab. Alok mutely pointed to the microscope.

'I don't believe it!' she exclaimed, looking at the brain through the microscope. It was like a vacuum cleaner had cleaned up all the protein deposits – a feature of a dementia-ridden brain. Could they have discovered a way to reverse dementia in the human brain?

The duo ran the tests again to be doubly sure, and sent the results to Vijayalakshmi's collaborator in Canada to have it tested by another lab. Finally, they were convinced that the observations were valid and published the results. 'The plant extract enhances the ability of the blood to target the harmful molecules in the brain and reverse dementia,' the published study concluded.

I spy another brain scientist who uses mice for research. Name the chapter and the scientist.

____

____

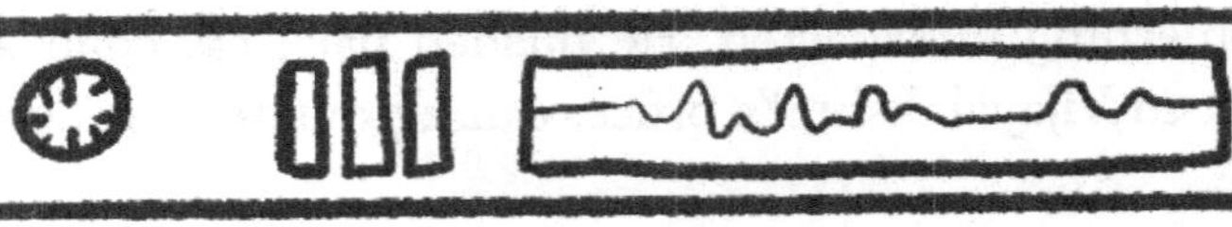

MOUSE IN THE HOUSE!

Vijayalakshmi uses mice in her experiments. But the first time she touched a mouse, it did not go too well. During her postdoctoral research, she was asked to go to the animal room and bring back a mouse. As soon as she picked one up, it leapt out of her hands and onto the ground, scuttling behind some instruments. She had no idea how to catch the runaway mouse!

In a panic, she rushed out of the animal room and called for help. A janitor happened to be around and came to her rescue. He caught the mouse and put it back into Vijayalakshmi's shaky hands. It's been 30 years since that incident; the scientist is now an expert at handling mice for research!

HORRIBLE HAIKU

Pop a pill
A memory rushes
Back into
sluggish brain

Today, Vijayalakshmi heads the Centre for Brain Research at IISc, where she continues her research on the ageing brain, including on dementia. The scientist is the recipient of many awards, including the Shanti Swarup Bhatnagar Prize, the Om Prakash Bhasin Award and the JC Bose Fellowship. But for Vijayalakshmi, the biggest reward is the thrilling work of studying the human brain.

'Science is hard. Lab work is back-breaking. You have to stand for hours and work 12 hours every day. It's not easy. You need a lot of determination,' she says. However, even at the age of 66, Vijayalakshmi is passionate about her research. 'Science is the search for truth,' she exclaims with a twinkle in her eye. 'Every day is a new challenge. But I look forward to unravelling the mysteries of the brain. It's pure joy!'

Colour Your Brain

Name the different parts of the human brain and colour them bright!

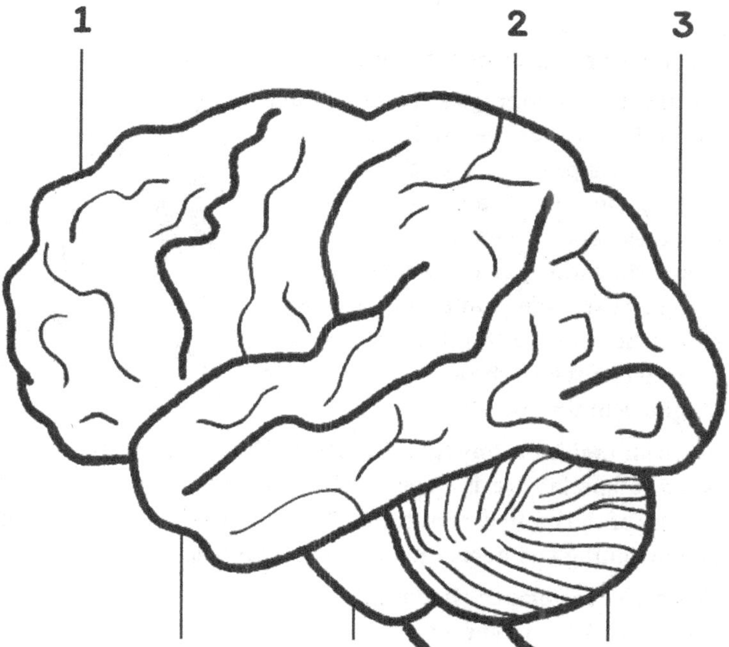

1 ______________________

2 ______________________

3 ______________________

4 ______________________

5 ______________________

6 ______________________

VOYAGE INTO THE BRAIN

Scientists use different types of machines to study the brain.

Electroencephalography (EEG): Small metal discs called electrodes are placed on the scalp to record the electrical activity in the brain. An EEG test observes and records these signals. Every time the person whose brain is being tracked does something, the brain signal becomes different. Doctors and scientists analyse these observations to diagnose brain disorders.

Positron emission tomography (PET): This is an imaging test where a special dye is injected into the body, after which the activity of the brain is monitored. The scan reveals how the brain is functioning and helps find any abnormalities.

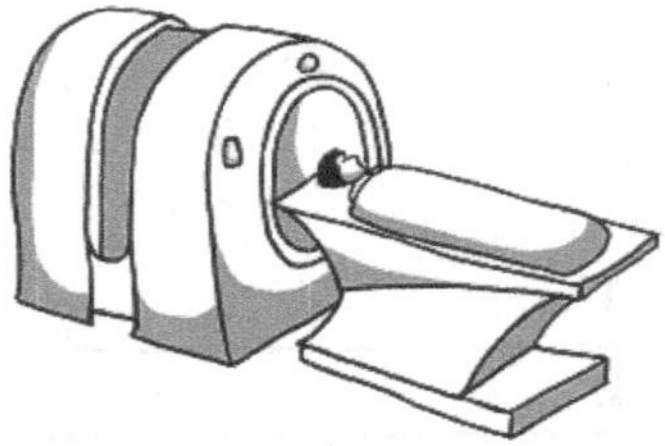

Magnetic resonance imaging (MRI): This is a type of scan that uses magnetism and radio frequency waves to differentiate between grey matter, white matter and cerebrospinal fluid. The print it generates is used by scientists and doctors to detect brain tumours, injuries and other abnormalities.

4

A Protein That Smashes Cancer Cells

The first time Sanjeev Das saw a cancerous cell under a microscope, he knew it would become his life's work. The tiny cell was uncontrollable! It split into two, and then became a bunch of cells within a few minutes. It spread, growing faster and faster, becoming a multitude of cells right before his eyes. It divided, multiplied and grew endlessly. It was nature gone wrong. There was no stopping the cancer cell.

Overwhelmed, he rose from the laboratory bench and went for a walk to clear his head. It was 1999, and Sanjeev was doing his doctorate at IISc, Bengaluru, in the microscopic world of biochemistry. At the time, cancer was one of the biggest causes of human deaths in the world. The deadly disease caused abnormal cells to grow uncontrollably, crowding out and destroying healthy cells. How could he stop these cells from growing, he wondered. As he wandered through the serene IISc campus, he resolved to find solutions to fight cancer with his research work.

Both chemistry and biology were among Sanjeev's favourite subjects when he was in high school. Every Thursday, the 15-year-old would look forward to his post-lunch science lab period. When most of his sleepy classmates zoned out after lunch, Sanjeev would sit in front of the science teacher and observe each experiment carefully. He watched the colours of liquids change as they underwent different chemical reactions; he mixed various substances to create entirely new substances; and he spent hours with a microscope, peering at an onion skin. Through the lens of chemistry and biology, the world seemed fascinating.

Like his friends, Sanjeev wanted to become a doctor, engineer or even a policeman in high school. But as life would have it, he found himself studying chemistry to start with. Before he knew it, he was doing his postgraduate degree in biochemistry at Calcutta University, where he was exposed to both chemistry and biology. He decided to continue studying and become a researcher who discovered new things.

At IISc, Sanjeev studied cervical cancer and discovered a therapeutic agent that could help in its treatment. By the time he was wrapping up his Ph.D, Sanjeev had become interested in the elusive 'p53 gene' as a possible game changer. The protein family p53 was a gene that was also called 'tumour suppressor' because it helped control the growth of human cells.

Sanjeev knew that cancer cells were cells that divided uncontrollably and ate up the nutrients of the body. These cells would then go on to affect healthy cells or create unusual growths that hurt internal organs. One of the reasons that abnormal cells kept dividing like that was because they did not have enough p53 protein to stop them.

'If I can get p53 to function normally in a cell, I can potentially cure most cancers in the world,' Sanjeev said to himself.

A lot of research had already been done on p53 and scientists had gleaned that p53 regulated how frequently healthy cells divided, how much energy they needed, and if they were damaged and had to be repaired. It signalled the cells on when it was time to die and when new cells needed to be born. But there were crucial aspects of p53 that had not been discovered that Sanjeev wanted to investigate. The big question that needed answering was how did p53 decide which cell was sick and had to die, and which could be saved? In other words, who was p53's boss?

Sanjeev did his postdoctoral research on this question at the Harvard Medical School in the USA for four years. There he came across new ways of studying proteins – a field called proteomics. Up until now, scientists had observed and studied a single protein and its genetic make-up. This took a long time to do. It also made it difficult to understand the interrelationships that proteins had with each other.

SCIENCE SPEAK
THE WONDEROUS BIOCHEMICAL WORLD

All living beings, including humans, have a variety of chemical reactions that go on inside their bodies. These reactions turn the food we eat into energy, which is then stored in the bonds between atoms and molecules. Yet another series of chemical reactions use this stored energy to build and grow cells* and help our bodies move.

*Like bricks are to a building, cells are the basic building blocks of all living things. Our bodies are made up of billions and trillions of cells that have been specially made to carry out different functions.

Using this new technique, scientists could study a group of proteins together and understand their connections.

'This is a bird's eye view of groups of proteins!' exclaimed an excited Sanjeev. He was convinced that this was the way to understand the p53 protein. By the end of his research, however, he had only found partial answers through proteomics about who ruled over p53.

In 2008, he returned to India and joined the National Institute of Immunology (NII) in New Delhi. He decided to tackle the p53 protein family with a different approach. The Yeast Two-Hybrid System*, better known as Y2H, was a biological technology used to study families of proteins by growing proteins on yeast. The technique was cheaper and faster than growing human cells.

Acquiring the Y2H system was a problem though. He could convince his institute to buy the technology, but India didn't have trained technicians to run the machine. For technical help, Sanjeev collaborated with a specialized laboratory in Australia. After the p53 samples grew on yeast in his lab in New Delhi, he would send them to the Australian lab. The technicians there would analyse the samples through the Y2H system and send back the results. The process was expensive, but this was the only way that Sanjeev could do the research that mattered to him.

*Yeast Two-Hybrid System or Y2H is now known as Two-Hybrid Screening.

WHY IS IT DIFFICULT TO CURE CANCER?

Cancer is unlike other diseases. It isn't caused by a virus, bacteria or external agents. Most cancers are caused by cells gone horribly wrong. Some cells inside the human body become cancerous and start growing at a maddening pace. These abnormal cells keep dividing, multiplying and growing inside a healthy human body eating away organs, affecting essential functions.

What's worse, these malignant cells grow alongside the healthy cells in a person with cancer. So any treatment that kills cancerous cells also kills off some healthy cells. This makes treating cancer hard.

Sanjeev's work in biochemistry is geared towards identifying how abnormal cells are different from healthy ones. In the future, this will help develop medicines for cancer which will only target the abnormal cells and spare the normal ones. This is called precision medicine.

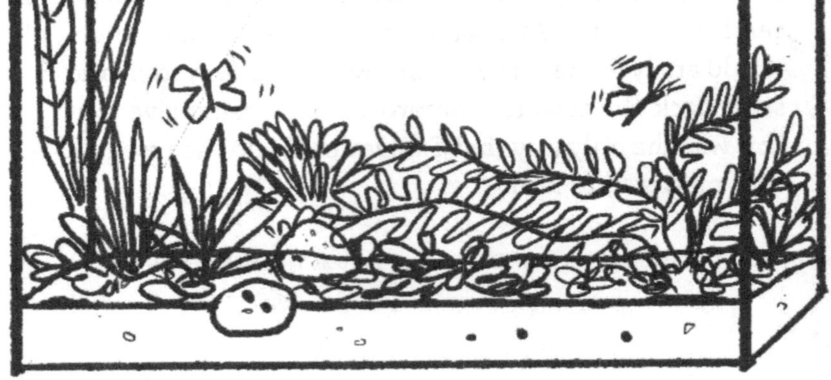

For the next three years, his team of six students worked on the project round the clock. But in the summer of 2010, Sanjeev hit a roadblock. Some of his yeast samples were damaged after a power outage in his lab. Adding to his troubles, he received discouraging news from the Australian lab about the recent batch of samples they had sent across. 'The results are just not conclusive,' he explained to his students.

It had been three years and all the research they had conducted so far had led to a dead end. 'We will have to try something new,' he said to his disappointed students.

Sanjeev was dismayed and frustrated, but he knew that he couldn't give up just yet. He decided to study p53 through chemistry instead of biology. He ditched the yeast system and zeroed in on a chemistry-based technology called mass spectrometry, which would allow him to study the proteins by their chemical processes.

There was a further change in plans. 'We need to look at p53 in human cells and not in yeast ones,' he told his students. Growing human cells in a laboratory was not easy. Sanjeev and his students had to make huge changes to their laboratory. Compared to yeast cells, human cells could be easily infected by bacteria and viruses. To grow them, a sterile chamber, which had a continuous flow of air, had to be created. The small, closed chamber had to be lit with UV light, so that no virus or bacteria could grow on the cells.

Inside it, they kept the cells in special plastic containers filled with a liquid or gel, called a growth medium.

I spy a biologist who dives deep into the cell to understand its oldest inhabitant. Name the biologist and the chapter in which they appear.

____

____

As the cells grew, they attached themselves to the walls of the plastic container. The process of scooping the p53 protein out of these cells was quite cumbersome as well. For each extraction, Sanjeev would sterilize his hands with alcohol, wear gloves, put his hands into the chamber and carefully open a container. Using a scalpel, he would scrape a bunch of cells from the edge of the container.

These extracted cells would then be put under a microscope. Special chemicals were added to break open the cells. Next, he would scratch the surface of the cell, as the p53 protein was hidden inside its nucleus. Once ruptured, he could finally extract the protein from inside the cell.

Each plastic container could only provide a few micrograms of proteins. To be fed into the mass spectrometry machine, they had to make 50 milligrams of p53. This meant that they had to collect protein for five to six months from a hundred containers!

Finally, the first batch of p53 was ready to be dispatched for further testing. Since India did not have skilled technicians who could work the mass spectrometry machine, Sanjeev sent the samples to a US-based laboratory.

Unfortunately, the first batch went bad. Somewhere in the process of harvesting the protein, the cells had gotten infected.

'The data is incorrect,' said Nirmalya Sen, one of Sanjeev's students.

'We have done something wrong. Our cell culture and isolation of protein needs to be perfect. Let's start again,' insisted Sanjeev.

For two years, their batches went bad twice and they had to start the cell culture again. Things didn't get any easier after fresh results came back from the American lab. The data consisted of long sheets of computation, which needed to be studied by data analysts – people who specialize in looking at information. Sanjeev and his team told the analysts what to look for in the reams of information. The analysts scoured through the data, pulled out the relevant bits and sent it back to the scientists.

Sanjeev and his team would then look at the results, match it with what scientists already knew about the p53 protein and check for new information and findings. Towards the end of 2012, when a fresh set of results arrived from the US, Sanjeev detected something unusual.

'Looks like the p53 protein has a role in the metabolic functions of the cell!' he told Nirmalya, staring at the results.

Scientists had already found that if a normal human cell was starved of energy, then the p53 protein was activated. However, Sanjeev and his group were the first to show that the protein had a role to play in the metabolic* functions of cells as well.

'Once p53 gets triggered under starvation conditions, it also changes the metabolic processes inside the cell,' wrote Sanjeev in his paper. However, the basic question still lingered – who tells p53 to destroy a cell or save it?

The answer came two years later, buried in a fresh mound of data sent back by the US lab. Sanjeev discovered the role of an enzyme† linked to p53. 'Look at this,' he said to Nirmalya. 'This enzyme – HDAC5 – interacts with the protein every time p53 decides whether to save the cell or let it die.'

'So when HDAC5 binds itself to p53, it means that the cell will survive...' Nirmalya responded.

*Metabolism is the set of chemical reactions in the cells of the body that change food into energy.

†An enzyme is a kind of protein in a cell that is responsible for chemical reactions inside the cell.

Batty cat cracks

Mr Medicine Man, Batty wants to know the name of the protein that causes all those rats in Batty's neighbourhood to become fat and slurpily juicy.

'...and when HDAC5 moves away from p53, it means that the damage to the cell is serious and p53 will destroy the cell,' completed Sanjeev.

They were excited! This discovery clearly revealed what was directing p53 to act on abnormal cells. He had finally found the boss of the p53 protein family!

Sanjeev's research opened up a whole new world in cancer therapy. Finally, medicines that targeted only the abnormal cells could be developed. This charted a new path towards developing precision medicine for cancer. Sanjeev was awarded the Shanti Swarup Bhatnagar Prize for his pathbreaking work in 2017.

HORRIBLE HAIKU

A biochemist
Smashes cancer
In spite of
unyielding yeast

Since then, Sanjeev's work in cancer biology has moved in a new direction. His laboratory now studies three new proteins that help metabolize sick cancer cells. Right now, he is studying PKM2, a metabolism enzyme, IDH1 and ATP-citrate lyase, a fat-breakdown protein.

'I hope I can find a chemical to block the function of these three proteins,' says Sanjeev to the researchers in his lab. That way, he believes that he can smash the cancer cells inside the human body without hurting the healthy ones. Here's to that!

Mind-blowing Accidental Discoveries

Sanjeev found the answers he was seeking thanks to a new technology called the mass spectrometry machine, which enabled him to look at proteins in a completely different way. Through the ages, scientists have discovered a bazillion things because of advances in technology. These technologies help them observe the world differently and further our scientific knowledge. However, sometimes, a scientist discovers mind-blowing things quite by accident. Match the following accidental discoveries with the scientists who discovered them.

A. In 1859, Robert Chesebrough noticed some workers complaining about rod wax, an annoying, waxy substance that gummed up their drilling equipment. He found that it treated cuts and burns. It is now a staple in every household.	1. PLASTIC
B. In 1945, at the end of World War II, Percy Spencer, an engineer, was looking for ways to use magnetron, which generated energy for radar systems. While he stood next to the device one day, a chocolate bar in his pocked melted.	2. CORN FLAKES
C. In 1870, Thomas Adams was experimenting with 'chicle', the sap gum from a South American tree, as a substitute for rubber. When he failed, he popped a piece into his mouth. He loved it.	3. PETROLEUM JELLY
D. In 1907, Belgian chemist, Leo Baekeland, was trying to find a replacement for shellac, an expensive resin secreted by a South Asian beetle. In order to invent this resin artificially, he combined formaldehyde with phenol and much to his surprise created a non-conductive, heat-resistant polymer.	4. THE MICROWAVE
E. While experimenting with cereal recipes in 1895, Will Keith Kellogg forgot about some boiled wheat that he had left sitting out. The wheat became crunchy and flaky.	5. CHEWING GUM

5

An Automatic Way to Do Mathematics

It was a bright, sweltering day in the month of May in 1997. The city of Kanpur was in siesta mode, preparing for the onset of a hot summer. The hostels and roads in the IIT campus were almost empty, and most of the students had left for the holidays. The ones left behind were busy making travel plans.

Manindra Agrawal, a professor at the department of computer science and engineering at IIT Kanpur (IIT-K), was the only one in a hurry. He cycled furiously towards the computer science building, his head in a whirl.

Just a couple of hours ago, he had been lounging about in the library, looking forward to a quiet session of reading. Exams had just ended. There were no classes to take, and no more students to guide or advise. He was free to do what he loved to do most – read mathematical journals!

The very first scientific paper he started on made him roll the journal up, pack it into his bag and rush to his bicycle. He parked his cycle outside the computer science building and headed to the professors' lounge. On the far end of the room, his colleague Somenath Biswas was relaxing with a newspaper and a cup of chai.

'Somenath!' Manindra called out. 'Look at this!' He shoved the rolled-up journal under Somenath's nose.

Used to his colleague's eccentricity, Somenath opened it to look at what Manindra was pointing at. He frowned at his excited friend, who was hovering like a spaceship desperate to land. Getting the hint, Somenath began to read. A few minutes later, he looked up, his eyes shining.

'They've used a different probabilistic algorithm to solve their equation! How interesting,' he remarked. (A probabilistic algorithm could help mathematicians find proofs faster. However, the results were not 100 per cent accurate. In mathematics speak, they were 99 per cent accurate.)

'This approach is unique,' agreed Manindra. 'It reduces errors in calculations.'

The approach was an interesting method to develop a proof. The two mathematicians discussed how they could use a similar probabilistic algorithm to solve some of the big mathematical puzzles that hadn't been cracked so far. They spent months looking for the right problem to solve.

Somenath was just finishing teaching a class at the start of the next semester a few weeks later, when Manindra burst into the classroom.

'Somenath, let's do primality testing,' he declared.

His colleague stared at him. Every mathematician was aware of the problem of 'primality testing'. It was notoriously difficult to solve and had baffled the best mathematical brains. On the surface, it was simple. The algorithm to solve it had to do just one thing: determine if a number – any number – was a prime number or not.

However, finding an equation that could emphatically decide if a number was prime or not had been an impossible quest for mathematicians. Somenath knew that Manindra's idea of finding a probabilistic algorithm that reduces error for primality testing was ambitious. He thought for a bit, nodded and then offered Manindra a piece of chalk.

For a year, the two scientists sat in empty classrooms, writing down equations on blackboards, brainstorming, correcting each other's work and suggesting alternative ideas.

In 1998, they created a reduced-error probabilistic algorithm that could solve primality testing with 99 per cent accuracy. What had foxed mathematicians for decades was cracked by two IIT-K professors. Excited, the duo wrote a paper about their approach and had it published. Scientists from around the world congratulated them on their success.

But Manindra continued to work on primality testing. 'Let's eliminate the probability from it now,' he told Somenath. He wanted to create a proof that was 100 per cent accurate – even 99 per cent wouldn't do. Somenath, however, had begun working on another project, and so bowed out of the partnership.

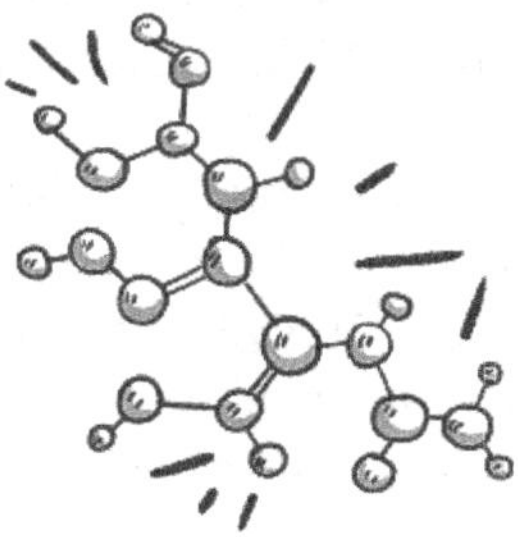

SCIENCE SPEAK

WHAT DO MATH GENIUSES DO?

If you like solving puzzles, you might like being a mathematician. Mathematicians develop theorems or proofs using rules of formal logic.

Mathematicians who work on developing proofs are basic scientists. They do not work on any application that is of direct use to society, like a product or service. Instead, they look for answers to the bigger questions of mathematics that might affect the way you live hundreds of years later. Manindra, for instance, is a mathematician who works on creating proofs. The results that mathematicians bring out are universal and once proved, they are always true – especially in a field of science such as physics or economics.

Applied mathematicians are another kind of maths geniuses who use these results to work on practical things. If you are one, you could help business organizations, the government, or other scientists in physics, economics, computer science and engineering with your skills. For example, using applied mathematics, you can figure out how many dogs in your neighbourhood may have rabies, or what the chances of you getting COVID-19 are. Or, how many older people in your apartment complex might need cataract surgeries.

Far from being boring, a mathematician can work in any of the cool fields listed below:
Logic, Number theory, Computation, Cryptography, Statistics, Probability, Game theory, Geometry, Numerical analysis

Can you find out what these terms mean? Research them online to check which one of them you find interesting.

HORRIBLE HAIKU

Colourful
chalkboard
A tough scientist
Doodling his brain

Manindra kept at it, day in and day out. He would finish work at the college and set out on long walks in the campus. As he walked, he would think and try out various solutions in his head. It was like arranging a complex jigsaw puzzle. You had to play with assorted pieces and try to make them fit. When they didn't, you either had to refit them or start over.

He knew he was looking for something that others thought impossible – an absolute proof to primality testing with complete accuracy. But Manindra had always liked clarity in his equations and felt he was close to a solution. 'I need to understand the structure of the problem, approach it from different angles and develop a deeper understanding of it,' he said aloud as he walked, his brain keeping pace with his brisk footsteps.

Hours spent on primality testing turned into months. Soon, his head was full of bits and pieces of the equation that he was trying to build. He would often stop mid-conversation and slip into a mathematical reverie. Friends and family knew that when Manindra drifted off with a faraway look in his eyes, he was busy solving equations on a blackboard inside his mind.

One evening, he was sitting for dinner with a bunch of friends, when an idea popped into his head.

'Mani, you're off again,' chided his wife.

'My brain is like the house I grew up in,' he joked.

Part of a big family, Manindra grew up in a large, rambling house in Prayagraj – a 25-room haveli, his ancestral home. Most of the rooms on the first floor were shut and unused. Manindra, his elder brother and their two cousins loved to play on this floor. They would secretly open a room and stumble onto something unexpected. Old photographs in a creaky drawer. A gramophone and old records. Musty clothes and plenty of cobwebs.

Mathematics was like this old haveli to Manindra. He would be sitting in a room full of people and his brain would fling open the door to an unused room, filled with images of equations, numbers, symbols and signs. A fresh idea or equation would beckon him as he stepped into the room, following its trail.

After four years, Manindra had still not found the proof for primality testing. But he didn't give up. He had scores of theories to try out and was busy building proofs to see if they worked. 'No research goes to waste,' he told himself. As a scientist he knew that 99.9 per cent of the time he would face failure, so he did not lose patience.

At the beginning of 2001, he knew he had hit a dead end and needed to find a new room in his brain with different ideas. A few weeks later, he decided to enlist the help of fellow researchers who could offer a fresh perspective. He called two of his students, Neeraj Kayal and Nitin Saxena, students of computer science at IIT-K, who were interested in working on the algorithm.

Batty cat cracks

What Batty wants to know is if Dr Maths here can calculate how many rats it takes to fill Batty's endless pit of a tummy. Is there a matherick amongst you who can develop a proof for this yummy equation? *Purr!*

The three of them sat in a classroom. Manindra got up, wrote something on the blackboard, then sat down. Nitin and Neeraj followed. One by one, they worked out possible equations that would fit into the proof. After working on it for a few months, they had a breakthrough. While their approach was new, it was a culmination of Manindra's work for the last three years.

'This might work!' he exclaimed.

'We should test this solution for numbers up to 10 billion,' said Nitin.

'We can build a programme for it,' said Neeraj.

Manindra agreed. Every possible solution had to be tested. Traditionally, mathematicians did all their calculations using the power of their own brains. But with computers, calculating with big numbers was easier. Nitin and Neeraj uploaded the equation into a computer and built a code to solve it based on Manindra's idea. They tested it for numbers up to 10 billion and found that the equation was working. The results had been 100 per cent accurate!

The three of them decided to formally work on a proof that they could publish and share with scientists worldwide. Again, this was not easy. Proving up to a limited number, even 10 billion, was doable. But how could you prove that the algorithm was true for all possible numbers? That given any number 'n', the algorithm would produce the right answer?

For six months, they worked on multiple equations to prove this. It was back to the blackboard in empty classrooms. One day, as Manindra was eating a meal with his wife, the last pieces of the jigsaw puzzle fell in place. His spoon stopped midway. He tuned in as the door to a new room opened in his mind, dumping equations all over its surface.

He grabbed the closest pen and jotted down the equations that had appeared in his head before they vanished! After years of hard work, he had finally done the impossible – he had solved primality testing! He met Nitin and Neeraj later that day. After they had readied the equations, the proof was published in the summer of 2002.

Their work was appreciated by mathematicians across the world. The unique algorithm was even named after them – the Agrawal-Kayal-Saxena primality test, or the AKS primality test. The three mathematicians received the Godel Prize, one of the biggest honours in the maths

Sleuth Snoop

I spy a physicist who found a turbulent point in clouds. Can you name them?

____

world, and the Fulkerson Prize. Manindra also received the Padma Shri, the Shanti Swarup Bhatnagar Award and the Infosys Prize for Mathematics.

Manindra's brain continues to dream up equations at the computer science and engineering department at IIT-K, where he encourages his students to deep dive into the unknown realms of mathematics. 'You need to aim higher,' he tells them. 'Be ambitious, try and solve a difficult...even impossible problem. Focus on doing mathematics, not on the results.'

All you maths geeks out there, be like Manindra, who keeps opening unexplored rooms in his mind so fresh insights and equations can saunter in.

Draw a Science Tree

If science is a tree and the various types of sciences are its branches, what will it look like? Add in the different branches below.

Hint: Start with physics, chemistry and biology. Don't forget to add sub-branches.

Done? Can you also add the scientists in the book and the fields they work in? Where do they fit on this tree?

6

A Way to Decode the Brain

Vidita Vaidya grew up on a lush green campus teeming with foxes, snakes, fruit bats, and even panthers and leopards. One day, when she was walking back home in the evening after playing with her friends, she saw a fox standing in front of her. Though she was used to the animals, it was the first time she had seen one this close.

Foxes have sharp teeth and can bite, Vidita realized. She froze in fear.

The fox froze too. They stared at each other – neither knew what to do. Then, little Vidita felt her brain jolt and she began to run. The fox did the same, scuttling into the bushes.

The incident stayed with Vidita through her childhood. She remembered feeling a zing of something shoot through her when she first saw the fox. This was adrenaline, she found out later – a chemical that the brain releases to increase blood circulation when the body is stressed or in danger. Vidita had felt fear at the idea of facing a dangerous animal with sharp teeth. But how had her brain signalled her body to freeze?

She continued to ponder over these questions as a graduate student of life science and biochemistry at St. Xavier's College, Mumbai. When she tried to find the answers, she hit a wall. Not much was known about the human brain and how the circuits inside this efficient machine worked when it came to strong emotions like fear. Did our brains change when we were sad, crying, angry, stressed, afraid or just happy, Vidita wondered.

This quest led her to the USA when she was 21 years old, for a postgraduate and doctoral degree in neuroscience. Vidita plunged into her research on how our brains react to stress at Yale University.

To get to the bottom of the mystery, she began running experiments on laboratory mice. Why did she choose to study the minds of mice rather than people? The answer is simple – the brain of a mouse responds to stress in a similar way to that of a human.

Luckily for her, she wasn't freaked out by mice. In fact, she quite liked handling them, which was a good thing, because they were going to play a starring role in her research for years to come. After experimenting on hundreds of mice, Vidita began to understand the impact that experiences of danger, fear and trauma have on mice (and our) brains.

Almost a decade later, in the year 2000, the neuroscientist returned to India and joined the Department of Biological

HORRIBLE HAIKU

Cold laboratory
A tiny brain
scuttles
Chasing the mouse

Sciences at the Tata Institute of Fundamental Research (TIFR), Mumbai. Here, she set up her own laboratory dedicated to studying the neurological circuitry of emotion and how it changed because of life experience.

Every morning, Vidita would head to her lab, which was situated at the very end of the TIFR campus, overlooking the sea. Her lab had sloping tin roofs and was always cool inside because they had to keep the air conditioning running for the mice. (That was a boon in the Mumbai heat!) From the outside, the laboratory looked quaint. Inside, it was chaos. The whitewashed walls were hidden under a mish-mash of paintings, notes and whiteboards filled with scribbles. All this was the work of Vidita's students, who did research with her on mice. The laboratory also had daydreaming corners, with beanbags and sofas for quick naps, a microwave to heat food and benches and tables to experiment upon. The tables were always overloaded with instruments.

But the most important part of the lab was, of course, the laboratory mice. The lab had two separate, enclosed black boxes with dim light and cameras installed. Vidita and her team of 10–12 students would run experiments on the mice. They would inject the mice with a drug, and leave them inside the box.

WHY ON EARTH DO SCIENTISTS STUDY MICE?

Who uses a mouse for scientific research? Well, a lot of scientists! The laboratory mouse is a small mammal used in biological and genetic research across the world. These mice are bred for the laboratory and belong to a species called *Mus Musculus*, or the house mouse.

Humans and mice have similar organs and physical responses; there are even cellular and genetic similarities. Our brains and theirs respond to medicines in the same ways. Scientists test new drugs and medication on mice before trying them on humans. Testing drugs or a medical treatment on animals is called a preclinical trial and is an important part of the scientific process.

Mice are also inexpensive and small in size (unlike elephants!), and are mild-tempered and docile. 'Mice have shorter lifespans, so I can genetically trace them, parent to child, modify their brains, and track them for generations,' says Vidita.

The camera would record their behaviour so that every minute change could be observed by the scientists. The results were intriguing – their overall behaviour did change visibly if they were feeling emotionally stressed, fearful or happy.

After years of research, Vidita has built models of how our brains are affected not just by stress, but also mental illness, sadness, grief or trauma experienced as children.

Much to her astonishment, Vidita has found that all our brains are unique in their circuitry. Each of us develops different strategies to respond to emotional issues and events that stress us. You might have been like your parents when you were a baby, but as you grow, your brain becomes your own. It develops a distinct wiring that is special to you, with its own impressions,

Batty has already applied for a permanent position at the laboratory of Dr Brain as a mouse catcher. It's Batty's dream job!

Sleuth Snoop

I spy another scientist named Vijayalakshmi in this book. How is her work similar to Vidita's?

____

____

____

____

____

patterns, reactions and colouring. Her work in neuroscience has led to important discoveries – like how to make medicines that treat depression* work faster.

To honour her amazing scientific contributions, Vidita has been awarded the prestigious Shanti Swarup Bhatnagar Prize. Though she has uncovered some of the mysteries of the neuroscience of emotions, there is so much more that she wants to know about the spectacular human brain. To do this, she continues to experiment on mice.

*Depression is a mood disorder that causes pervasive feelings of sadness, hopelessness and loss of interest in life.

THE CASE OF THE MISSING MICE

Though Vidita is good at handling mice, the skill doesn't come easily to most scientists. At the TIFR lab, it is a regular occurrence for a mouse to run out of the box. Panicky students then spend the entire day looking for it!

One day, a mouse hopped off the table and hid behind the wires. Vidita calmly asked her student to shut the door of the lab, so that the creature would not escape. Instead, the frightened student dashed out of the room and banged the door shut, leaving Vidita to deal with the runaway mouse. Over the years, Vidita has learnt to be gentle with her furry animal subjects. 'If you're scared or nervous, they sense that and run away or bite you,' she says.

Test your Brain Quotient

How sharp is your brain? How does it compare to your friends? Test your friends quickly with the memory game, 'What's Missing'.

What you need

- Tray or plate
- 10-20 small items, like an eraser, pencil, coin, marble, seed, magnet, etc.
- Cloth or towel to cover the tray
- Two friends for the game

Instructions

Spread out all the items on a tray. Ask your friends to look at all the items for 30 seconds. Cover the tray with a cloth, hiding everything.

Then, ask them to shut their eyes. Remove one item from the tray. Ask them to open their eyes and remove the cloth covering the tray. Ask them, 'What is missing?' Can they guess what you removed?

Try the game again by giving your friends more time to view all the items. Try the game with less time. Play the game again with more items on the tray or with fewer items. Next, don't show your friends what's missing. Let them close their eyes, feel all the objects and decide what's missing without looking.

Write down the results for all variations of the game. What did you find out?

The Brainy Quiz

		TRUE	FALSE
1	The average human brain is made up of up to 80% water.		
2	Your brain is 9% of your total body weight but uses 35% of your body's energy.		
3	After age 30, the brain shrinks by exactly .25% in mass each year.		
4	The brain feels more pain than the rest of the body.		
5	The energy used by the brain is enough to light a 25 watt light bulb.		
6	Humans have the most complex brain out there.		
7	The right side of your brain controls the left side of your body, while the left side of your brain controls the right side of your body.		
8	Your skull is made up of 28 bones.		
9	The human brain weighs about as much as a Chihuahua.		
10	When we laugh eight different areas in our brain are in action.		
11	The human brain is so soft that a table knife would be more than enough to slice through it.		
12	Learning two languages before age five strengthens the brain.		
13	Every time you recall a memory or have a new thought a new connection is made.		
14	The brain is the fattiest part of the body, with a fat content of around 60%.		
15	The brain can stay alive 1–3 minutes without any oxygen.		

7

A Hammer to Break a Cell Wall

Manjula Reddy is quite fond of the Escherichia coli or E. coli, which is a type of bacteria. The bacteria lover is the chief scientist at the Centre for Cellular and Molecular Biology (CCMB) in Hyderabad, where her day starts and ends with observing these single-celled organisms. A microbiologist and a bacterial geneticist who studies microscopic life forms for a living, she has been studying this fascinating bacterium for the last 35 years and knows a lot about it.

It has been known for a long time that E. coli and humans share an intricate relationship. Mostly harmless, the bacteria live in the human intestine and help keep our digestive tracts* healthy. Some other E. coli, however, are disruptive and cause diarrhoea and tummy infections. Another odd fact that scientists

*The digestive tract is made up of organs that food and liquids travel through when you eat or drink something. These include the mouth, throat, oesophagus, stomach, small intestine, large intestine, rectum and anus.

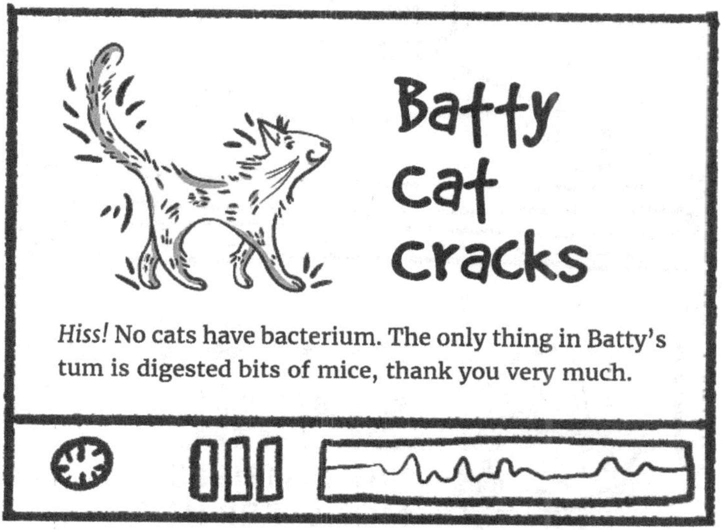

Hiss! No cats have bacterium. The only thing in Batty's tum is digested bits of mice, thank you very much.

know about this bacterium is that it grows really fast. When there is enough food, it can grow from a single cell to one billion overnight!

The E. coli comes in assorted shapes and forms. While it looks like a thin rod when it is little, it turns into a rectangular room as it gets longer and fatter! The way it grows is peculiar. It isn't stretchable. Rather, it breaks its cell walls as it grows and adds more cell wall material to make itself bigger. Every morning, Manjula goes straight to her laboratory and peers through the microscope, wondering which new part of itself the bacterium will reveal to her.

As a kid, Manjula didn't know that she would be spending her life observing a super-tiny, single-celled microbe, which is essentially 100 times thinner than a single strand of hair. But she did know that she wanted to become a scientist.

SCIENCE SPEAK

THE INVISIBLE MONSTERS IN YOUR BELLY

Bacteria are tiny organisms made of single cells that are invisible to the human eye. We can't see them without a microscope as they're 1,000 times smaller than a pencil tip!

Sneaky bacteria live everywhere. They are in the soil, air and water, on rotis and vegetables, on the countertops of bathrooms, kitchen taps, and in your nostrils and eyelashes. However, their favourite place to live is inside our bodies (yikes!). Each human body, including yours, is home to millions of tiny living organisms. Scientists call them microbes. Did you know that you have more microbes living in your body than you have human cells?

Bacteria are a type of microbe. (Other microbes include yeast, fungi, algae and protozoa.) We carry them with us wherever we go. We feed them and help them grow. From the day we are born, we carry them in our noses, mouths, and on our skin, but especially in our bellies and intestines. In turn, these bacteria help us stay healthy.

Most of the microbes found in human bodies are the good ones. The good bacteria on the skin, and in the mouth and nose, fight the bad bacteria that want to enter our body. The bacteria in our stomachs break down food and milk and help us digest what we eat. The ones that live in our intestines produce vitamins B12 and K, which our cells cannot produce on their own. More than 1,000 types of bacteria live in our gut!

Would you like to say thank you to the good bacteria in your stomach? Well, do not eat sugary things today. These microbes don't like cakes, biscuits, brownies, white bread or burgers. Their favourite foods are fibre from beans, chickpeas, cereals, seeds and veggies. Called prebiotics, they help the microbiota grow and thrive.

It was when she was a postgraduate student at the University of Hyderabad, that she first saw an E. coli up close in the laboratory.

Under the microscope, the E. coli showed up as a thin, elongated rod-shaped organism. 'They look like rectangular rooms,' said Manjula to her teacher. Her teacher was surprised. 'Who thinks of a single-celled invisible organism as a room?' she asked.

Manjula started growing E. coli in the laboratory. She took a platinum loop and heated it with a flame to sterilize it. Using the loop, she scooped up the E. coli from a dish and put it into another Petri dish, where she fed the bacteria a mix of salt and sugar. Then, she sat back and watched the E. coli grow and multiply. One became 10, which became a few hundreds in the next 12 hours. She observed it under the microscope and was convinced that each bacterium did look like a rectangular room!

Four years later, Manjula had gotten so attached to the E. coli that she knew she would spend the rest of her working years studying it. But before she could do a doctoral degree or Ph.D, she got married and started a family. Her dream of becoming a microbiologist and scientist was postponed as she travelled with her husband.

In 1990, when Manjula turned 24, she returned to Hyderabad and joined CCMB as a junior scientist. She was delighted to be looking at her favourite bacteria again! Under the microscope, the E. coli continued to look like a small room to Manjula. It would grow bigger

HORRIBLE HAIKU

A single shell
An invisible
hammerhead
Breaks the wall
Birthing new cell

and bigger till it split into two E. coli and then four. Rapt, she watched in fascination.

After getting a Ph.D in 2002, the molecular biologist set up her own lab at the CCMB in 2007 to explore the idea of E. coli as a room. At this time, most scientists who were studying the bacteria were focused on creating antibiotics that targeted its cell wall. But no one had figured out just how the cell walls grew. Manjula knew the answer to this mystery lay in the bacteria's cell walls.

'Every time the bacterium wants to grow, the room's walls need to increase in size,' Manjula explained to her team. Though the bacterium looked like a rod, its walls were not stretchable. Every time it got bigger, the walls had to be broken down. To do this, a micro-hammer, invisible to the eye, had to be used to break the wall of the cell. This would make space for new bricks to rebuild the wall, and create more room so that the bacteria could grow.

The question Manjula wanted to understand was this – how did the hammer know when to break the wall to expand the room? She found that a space-making protein called hydrolase acted as the hammer for the cell.

SCIENCE SPEAK

EVERYBODY LOVES THE E. COLI

Earth is home to billions of different kinds of bacteria. However, only a few, like E. coli, are popular with microbiologists, geneticists and scientists. This well-known bacteria was discovered by a German-Austrian paediatrician named Theodor Escherich, who found it in the faeces of his patients who suffered from diarrhoea. Apart from finding the exact cause for the stomach upset in his patients, he also found that the bacteria was rather easy to grow in a lab.

E. coli are now a favourite with microbiologists as they offer valuable insights into humans and mammals. Anything true of E. coli cells will probably be true of humans and other mammals like elephants, scientists concur.

Hundreds of E. coli can grow on a *single* grain of salt! A single bacterium on a nutritious jelly can produce millions of its own kind in just 24 hours. Since the bacterium splits and is born faster, it is easy to observe the daughter cell of an E. coli and even follow multiple generations under a microscope. Another reason why scientists love this bacteria is that the temperature they grow at is a comfortable 37.4° Celsius – easy to create in the laboratory.

Bacteria are also shape-shifters. They regularly change shape and size. When you give the bacterium less food or the temperature gets too high, it increases in length, becoming a rope-like structure, forms long chains or develops into an L-shape. Observing this, microbiologists and geneticists can understand a lot about cell growth and how deformities occur in living organisms.

The E. coli samples that Manjula was using in her laboratory in Hyderabad came from the faeces of a patient in the USA who lived there in 1925. Yes, you read that right. Easy to grow, safe to observe and able to change into many things, it makes for the perfect laboratory pet. No wonder Manjula is enamoured.

Sleuth Snoop

I spy a biologist who peeks into cancer cells. Name them and the field they work in.

____

____

The protein was an enzyme* that was responsible for expanding the room by breaking the bonds in the cell wall and increasing its size. 'If we can stop the supply of hydrolase to the cell walls, the bacteria will stop growing,' she said.

Her team studied the E. coli's cell wall, day after day, for years. Slowly and painstakingly, they found out that only when new cement and new bricks were ready – that is, only when the food for the cell to grow was available – did the hammer, or the hydrolase, get into action mode and break the wall.

There was another important discovery that Manjula made. An unknown protein acted like a supervisor every time the cell wall was set to break.

*An enzyme is a biological catalyst. It speeds up the rate of a specific chemical reaction in the cell.

FOXY FACTS

ARE ANTIBIOTICS GOOD AND BAD?

Antibiotics are medicines prescribed by doctors to treat infections caused by harmful microbes. They kill bacteria and stop them from growing in the body. But there's a problem – the medicine targets not just the bad bacteria but the good ones as well. A majority of microbes living in our bodies are not just harmless but essential to maintaining our health and well-being.

People who take a lot of antibiotics may get sick because the medicines destroy the good bacteria too. With over usage, the bad bacteria learn to adapt and turn into mean 'superbugs'. These are resistant to antibiotics, so the infection can no longer be cured. In a nutshell, this is why you should take antibiotics only when prescribed by a doctor.

A PARASITE THAT HATES LABS

Sudha Bhattarcharya, who works at Jawaharlal Nehru University (JNU), is also a molecular biologist like Manjula Reddy. Just as Manjula studies E. coli, Sudha's first project was to explore the microscopic world of an amoeba called the *Entamoeba histolytica*. The parasite causes amoebiasis, an infection of the intestine which causes bloody dysentery, and can be life-threatening as it chews up tissue.

Sudha started researching this parasite in the 1980s, when the disease was widely prevalent and a huge problem in India.

Amoebas like eating bacteria, and bacteria, as you now know, are present in large numbers in human intestines. But unlike E. coli, *Entamoeba histolytica* is really hard to grow in laboratories. So Sudha visited the USA to learn how to grow it.

These bacteria thrive best in the human intestine, Sudha observed. To grow the amoeba, she first needed to procure a lot of hard-to-get nutrients. One of them was bovine blood. Since cow slaughter was banned in parts of India, she had to import the bovine serum from the USA. Even then, the amoeba was quite unresponsive, as it did not have the habitat of a human intestine to grow in. For example, it would refuse to grow if there was too much oxygen in the container. Sudha needed to make sure that the container had limited oxygen molecules.

Sometimes, her samples, which needed to be preserved in a frozen state at below -80° Celsius, were destroyed because of long power shutdowns, a frequent occurrence in the 1980s. Once, when there was no electricity for 24 hours, Sudha and her team bought dry ice and filled their freezers so the samples would not get spoiled.

Another requirement for growing the amoeba was that the medium had to be changed every three days. So Sudha couldn't take long holidays. As the amoeba grew, there were other challenges. She had to extract DNA from the parasite's cell to study it in her laboratory. In the beginning, the samples were wasted because as the scientist broke the cell to extract the DNA, she noticed that the DNA-breaking enzymes of the cell got activated and destroyed the DNA.

With great effort and care, Sudha succeeded in growing the amoeba and studying its DNA. She was among the first to do a DNA sequencing decades ago, and she found that many of the amoeba's DNA molecules were circular. 'We also found out that the amoeba has a lot of "jumping genes", which have jumped in different ways in the amoeba samples taken from humans in different parts of the world,' she wrote in her research paper.

Over the years, with more attention being paid to clean drinking water, the problem of amoebiasis has reduced in our country. Sudha has now retired from this project. Despite the hurdles, she feels the path of scientific discovery is rewarding. 'It is extremely satisfying to understand what we didn't know before,' she says.

This protein gave a signal to the hydrolase about when to break the wall. This supervisor, Manjula discovered, was yet another protein called new lipoprotein or nlpI. It sensed that the E. coli had enough nutrients around it and wanted to grow, and gave the green signal to the hydrolase to break the walls.

'If we can starve the cells by giving them no nutrients, the protein, nlpI, will not allow the cell to grow,' she said to her team.

Manjula's discovery is astounding. It signifies a breakthrough in the study of E. coli. Once scientists know how its cells walls grow and expand, they can create effective drugs to kill bad E. coli by focusing on reining in the hammer or the supervisor. Better drugs will mean quicker recoveries from an infection.

With her research, scientists can now develop drugs and antibiotics that can kill the bacteria even before it grows. They can also develop drugs that are effective on antibiotic-resistant bacteria. For this work, Manjula has been awarded the coveted Infosys Prize in Life Sciences.

Manjula continues to study her favourite bacteria. She realizes it is challenging work. Almost 99 per cent of the time, you face failure in research. However, it's all worth it for that 1 per cent chance of success. Manjula found success with her inspired ideas to find out more about the E. coli 'that looked like a room' and 'the hammer that broke the wall'. 'That elation on finding new things and discovering the secrets of how bacteria live and die is addictive. I'm ready to spend another 50 years in the laboratory, looking for more of nature's secrets,' she says.

Fill in the Bacteria

Below are the different types of bacteria in all their microscopic splendour. As you can see, they come in assorted shapes and sizes – bean-shaped, round, wavy and elongated. Draw and colour them into your body on the right and house as many types of bacteria as you can.

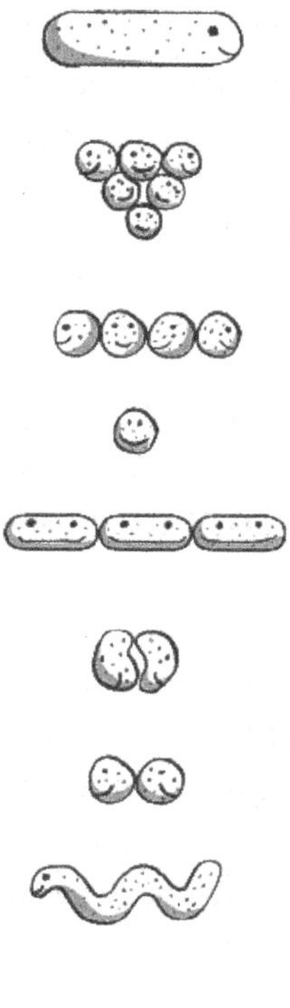

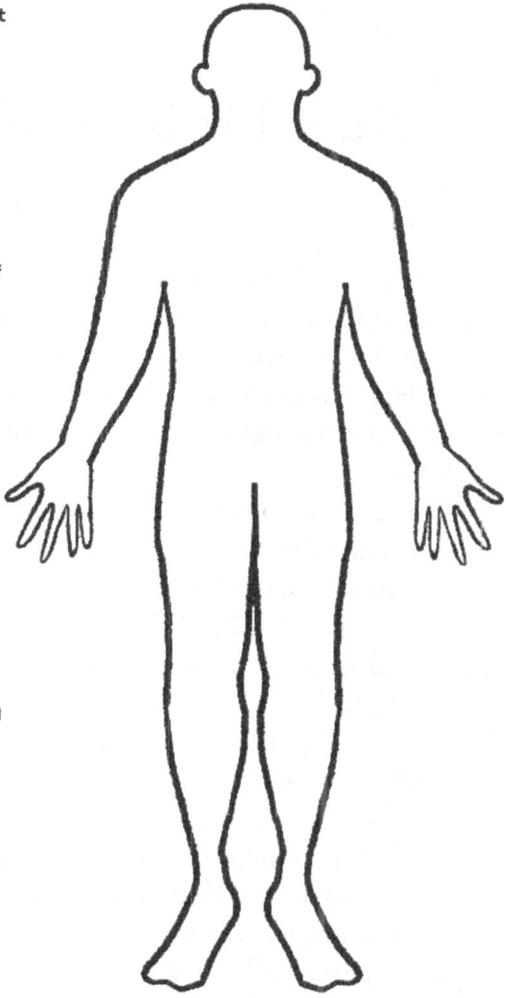

8

A New Field of Science

As a child, Mitali Mukerji loved to ask questions. Why did humans have two eyes when flies had so many? How did a gardener graft a cactus? How did wings form on birds? Her family, teachers, classmates, and even the school principal were subjected to her constant whys and hows.

'Why do you ask so many questions?' asked her grandmother one day.

'I'm just curious,' she replied.

Even in school, Mitali didn't stop asking questions. She would observe all the little and big things in the world around her – nature, people, machines and whatnot – and ponder on them. What made cars move? How did bees smell?

One day, her teacher helped her understand how important her inquisitiveness was. 'Look at anything carefully, and you will find a unique question there. It can be a big question or a small one, but it will be something that others do not know the answer to.

Having the determination to find answers to mysterious questions is how you become a scientist,' she explained.

Aha! Her incessant questions even had a name! She now knew that being curious was called having a 'scientific temper'. Mitali was thrilled and decided to become a scientist. That way, she could do all the things she loved the most – ask questions, be inquisitive and discover new stuff!

After graduating, she went to IISc in Bengaluru, where she earned a Ph.D in bacterial molecular genetics – a branch of science that deals with the genetics of bacteria.

At the institute, Mitali's research focused on E. coli. Her work was to pop open the bacteria cell and study what it was made of.

After completing her Ph.D in 1997, Mitali joined the Institute of Genomics and Integrative Biology (IGIB) in New Delhi, a government institute, which conducted cutting-edge research in genetics. She had fulfilled her lifelong dream – she was finally a scientist!

One day, when Mitali was visiting the neurology department at the All India Institute of Medical Sciences (AIIMS) in Delhi, she came across patients with spinocerebellar ataxia* (SCA). A genetic disease, it made patients (including children) lose control over their limbs.

*Spinocerebelllar ataxia (SCA) is a genetic disorder of the brain that causes loss of limb coordination in patients. People cannot control their feet, hands and even eye movements if they have this disease.

It's All in Your Genes!

Here are some elements that scientists studying genetics work with. Can you match the scientific term to its meaning?

SCIENTIFIC TERM	MEANING
1. GENETICISTS	A. A new kind of medicine which uses genetic engineering to treat a disease. It's still at an experimental stage.
2. GENOME	B. Basic units that carry information on personality, characteristics and diseases from parent to child
3. DNA	C. A branch of biology where scientists study how features pass on from parents to their children
4. GENETICS	D. A long molecule inside a cell that stores instructions. It's called deoxyribonucleic acid.
5. GENE THERAPY	E. Tiny structures inside cells made of protein. The information stored inside this is a recipe that tells a cell how to function.
6. CHROMOSOMES	F. People who study heredity and how genetic variations contribute to inherited characteristics
7. GENES	G. The complete set of genetic materials that one inherits from a parent

Sleuth Snoop

I spy another curious genius who probed E.Coli. Name the scientist and the chapter.

____

____

Wheelchair-bound, they couldn't walk as they couldn't control their legs.

Mitali wanted to investigate the genetic basis of this disease and what DNA changes caused it. She chose it as the focus of her work at the IGIB – the project would revolve around identifying the gene that caused SCA. Once the project was approved by IGIB's head, Samir Brahmachari, she visited AIIMS to collect spit and blood samples from SCA patients.

'Err...why are you collecting my gob?' asked a puzzled patient.

'Your saliva has 19,000 gene samples for me to study!' Mitali informed him.

Wide-eyed, he stared into the Petri dish that Mitali held out. He couldn't even see his spit in the transparent dish. 'With this sample, I can study your genes. If I compare them with the genes of humans who don't have SCA, I can find out which gene in your body caused this disease,' she explained.

As she worked on the SCA project, studying the genetic makeup of humans became her passion. Mitali hypothesized that if she could understand the Indian population through their genes, she could figure out which diseases were specific to us. 'If we can map out the Indian human genome, we can understand the basis of genetic diseases in our country,' Samir told her .

Together, with nearly 200 people across the country, they began a project called the Indian Genome Variation Consortium (IGVC), which was aimed at collecting and studying genetic samples of a cross section of Indians to find the genetic underpinnings of diseases specific to the population. Mitali hoped to find the answers to questions like why children had SCA and how they could manage it better. In the future, this database could also be used for gene therapy.

From 2003 to 2007, Mitali led the IGVC initiative and worked with scientists across the country to create a genetic map of India. She worked on many questions as she collected this data. Which genes were brought into India from which continents, and how? What made Indians...well, *Indians*? Was there anything in our genes that tied us together? Why were some people born sick while others healthy?

WEIRD AND WONDERFUL GENES

Genetics is a branch of biology in which scientists study how certain features and characteristics get passed on from parents to their children. Genes are essentially a record of all our features, which are present in every cell in the body. These records map our nature, personality, how we look, what talents we have inherited and the diseases we carry.

Do you have a dimple? That's because of a particular gene. Are your hair and eyes brown? Again, that's because of a gene. Using genetic studies, scientists can find out why some children are prone to allergies or if specific genes mean you can draw like Picasso.

Likewise, many diseases can be attributed to the presence of certain genes. Mitali's research, for instance, is specific to Indian genes and the diseases they carry. In the future, scientists will make medicines that target specific genes, a type of treatment called gene therapy. So if you have a disease in your genetic map, doctors in the future might be able to prescribe drugs using this therapy.

As she dug deep into the Indian gene pool, Mitali uncovered new information. She learned that a lot of us have a resistance gene which made us anaemic* as a population but also resistant to malaria. Another strange discovery was that Indian skin was thicker than usual as it offered added protection from an environment where parasites were more prevalent.

It was while making these remarkable discoveries that Mitali met Bhavana Prasher, a doctor and an expert in a completely different kind of science – Ayurveda.

Mitali saw a lot of parallels between genetic science and Ayurveda.

'This sounds very similar to my research. The concept of *prakriti* sounds like genetics,' Mitali told Bhavana.

Another interesting similarity was that genomics also aimed to tailor-make medicine according to the unique genetic makeup of a person. This opened up new scientific questions for Mitali. She wondered if she could find parallels and connections between the genetic maps of Indians and Ayurveda's theories and concepts. Was the *prakriti* of individuals also reflected at the level of their genetics? she asked herself.

Mitali and Bhavana decided to integrate Ayurveda and genetics! If ancient and modern medicine were combined, they hoped that they could find a way to prevent and treat diseases. The challenge was that all knowledge in Ayurveda was based on ancient texts.

*Anaemia is a condition in which the patient has less than the normal number of red blood cells, decreasing their blood's oxygen-carrying capacity.

HORRIBLE HAIKU

Spooky laboratory
Where scientists tweak
Genetic Indians

There were few scientific research papers or studies to follow. But Mitali and Bhavana were not deterred and started an unusual research centre in IGIB, which delved into the unknown world of what they named Ayurgenomics.

The aim was to use the genetic maps of Indians and find similarities between Ayurveda's concept of *prakriti* and what geneticists called genetic variation. They selected a group of random Indians to study. Bhavana prepared a questionnaire, which collected details about body frame, weight, skin, appetite, voice, eye colour and other environmental and psychological characteristics to determine a person's *prakriti*. Mitali analysed the genes of the same people, running biochemical tests.

As they expected, they discovered that there were genetic differences between different *prakriti* types and similarities within the same type. However, the scientific community was not convinced about the science behind Ayurgenomics. The duo's research papers were rejected by several journals. Some even called the mixture of modern genetics and ancient Ayurveda a pseudoscience*. But Mitali and Bhavana ignored their critics and continued to forge ahead.

*Pseudoscience relates to beliefs, practices or results that claim to be scientific and factual but have not gone through the scientific method.

FOXY FACTS

CRACKING THE DNA CODE

- Humans get 23 chromosomes from the mother and 23 from the father. We have exactly 46 chromosomes in each cell. These chromosomes are the instruction manuals that help decide if a person will have a long nose, curly hair and green eyes, or if they will be left-handed.
- All humans, be it from Asia, Africa or Europe, share 99.9 per cent of the same genetic material! It's the remaining, seemingly miniscule 0.1 per cent that gives us our unique attributes. It makes our hair colour, complexion, height and features different, and decides which diseases we are likely to get.
- If you unravel all the DNA molecules in the human body, they can form a pathway to travel to the sun and back many times over.

By 2008, they were tracking a critical gene, the EGLN1. A version of the EGLN1 was linked to a life-threatening sickness that occurred in high altitudes. They found that in Ayurveda, it was associated with *Kapha* people. But another version of EGLN1 helped *Pitta* people cope with less oxygen in their bodies. Their innovative research work was published in an international journal.

The published paper popularized Mitali and Bhavana's work. Geneticists and scientists across the country approached them, curious about Ayurgenomics. Thanks to her curiosity, an innovative field of science that had never been explored before has been developed! In 2010, Mitali received the Shanti Swarup Bhatnagar Award for her contribution to the field of medical sciences.

Today, Ayurgenomics is an accepted field of genetic study unique to India. There is an Ayurgenomics unit in IGIB with more than 30 people working with Mitali and Bhavana. Scientists at the institute are working to find more patterns of similarity between ancient Ayurvedic principles and modern genomics. Mitali is convinced that traditional medicinal systems can be understood through the lens of modern science. 'I do not understand Ayurveda fully but I am willing to test it with the methods of science,' she says. After all, if you are curious, you tend to ask all kinds of questions.

A chief scientist at the IGIB, Mitali's work in genetics remains her focus. She oversees her laboratory and students, collects blood samples, isolates DNA from these samples and puts them into gene-reading

Batty cat cracks

Meowrr! What's the big deal about a new science field? Me create many.

- Ratonomy: Art of creating juicy, fat rats
- Rarticle Science: Smash two mice to see what remains
- Sneakaviour: Studies and predicts the sneaky behaviour of rats

machines to analyse the data. Beyond her scientific acumen, she counts her questioning spirit and ability to make unlikely connections as her biggest assets.

'Becoming a scientist is easy,' she tells her students. 'The first thing you need is curiosity about the world around you. You need to be observant. Everything possesses something unique that you can ask a question about. It can be a big question or a small one. But there will definitely be something that others do not know the answer to, and that is how you start becoming a scientist...' she trails off, repeating the wise words of her school teacher.

HOW AYURVEDA WORKS

Ayurveda is a 5,000-year-old ancient Indian medicine system that treats humans according to their inherent physical and mental nature or *prakriti*. Ayurveda practitioners believe that humans are made up of five life forces or elements: air, space, water, earth and fire. Each person inherits a mix of these five forces, which determine their distinct physical, physiological and psychological features. There are three basic types of mixes or *dosha*s as they are called by Ayurveda physicians: *Vata dosha* (a combination of space and air), *Pitta dosha* (fire and water), and *Kapha dosha* (water and earth). The unique combinations of these *dosha*s determine the unique nature or *prakriti* of a person. Through the analysis of *prakriti*, Ayurvedic physicians diagnose disorders in an individual and suggest customized treatment.

Make Your own DNA

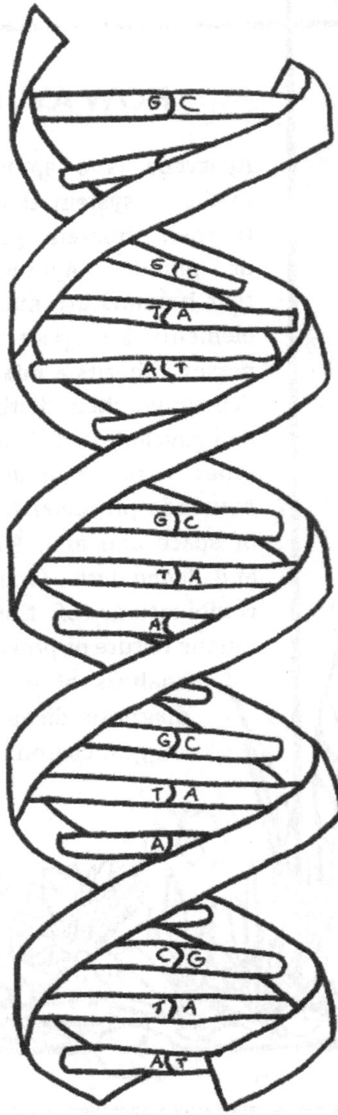

DNA is the building block of your physical features and personality. Colour this DNA with your personality. Use your favourite colours and describe your features and personality traits. For each feature, add in whom you got it from. Was it your father or his parents? Was it your mother or her parents?

1 ____________________

2 ____________________

3 ____________________

4 ____________________

5 ____________________

6 ____________________

7 ____________________

8 ____________________

9 ____________________

10 ____________________

11 ____________________

12 ____________________

13 ____________________

14 ____________________

15 ____________________

16 ____________________

17 ____________________

9

Equations for a Monsoon Cloud

It was the beginning of spring in 1999. Rama Govindarajan, a young scientist in the engineering mechanics unit of the Jawaharlal Nehru Centre for Advanced Scientific Research (JNCASR) in Bengaluru, was busy at work.

She had two students coming to intern with her during the summer break, and she wanted to make sure that she had enough work for them. That's when a third student, Balaji Ranganathan, from the Indian Institute of Technology, Madras (IIT-M), contacted her.

'Please, Professor,' he said, over the phone. 'I would like to do a project with you.'

Even though two students over one summer break was already too much to handle, Rama asked Balaji to come to her lab. She knew that dedicated and enthusiastic students were hard to find. As a scientist, she also wanted to encourage youngsters like Balaji to take up research. An internship was usually the first step for students to figure out if they liked doing research, and which field they wanted to explore.

Rama stayed back at the office that evening to finish her work. The sun had set and the rest of the staff had left for the day. Rama was used to working alone, as her days sometimes stretched from early in the morning to late into the night. She sat right through dinner time, trying to find the right project to assign Balaji for the next two months. She knew colleagues who had done interesting experiments in fluid instabilities*, a subject that she had also worked on. She decided to build a project based on this concept for Balaji to work on.

On the first day of his internship, Balaji could barely hide his excitement as he entered Rama's office.

'There is a process through which fluids† transition from laminar to turbulent (See Page 109),' said Rama. 'The research project I have chosen for you has to do with this.'

Rama's project for Balaji in fluid dynamics (the science of movement of liquids, gases and plasma) was technically advanced and challenging. He had to run a computer model where two types of fluids were flowing through a long channel, and calculate the flow speed at which the fluid flow would turn from a laminar flow which does not change in time to a flow which would contain waves and other disturbances (that is, calculate the speed at which the flow would go unstable). Balaji would need to constantly change the percentage of

*Fluid instability is a situation under which a liquid or gas changes from one kind of behaviour of flowing to another.

†A fluid is a physics term for a liquid or a gas. It's anything that is not a solid.

different fluids in the mix, run the computer program again, and do complex calculations.

In the simulation, he had to change the viscosity of the two fluids. Balaji found that even a minute change in the viscosity of one fluid could give dramatically different results. His assignment was to see how the results would vary with a 10 per cent change in different fluids, across different mixes. He kept changing the percentage, computed the results and noted down the differences.

Under Rama's guidance, Balaji sat for hours in front of his computer, running calculations. A month later, the intern came to her with the results. Rama frowned as she scanned them.

'This shows that if you changed the viscosity by 10 per cent, you can change the speed at which it goes to unstable or disturbed by a 1,000 per cent!' exclaimed Rama. The result sounded too spectacular to be true. 'This doesn't sound right. Check it again,' she said.

Balaji came back a week later with the same results. Rama sat up all night to recheck the calculations on her computer. She built an equation on the basis of the calculations and found that Balaji's results had been correct all along.

'We have found a singular perturbation*!' exclaimed Rama. What the two of them had found had never been discovered before. Their work proved that, in two fluids flowing together and slightly mixing with each other, if you changed the viscosity of one fluid by 10 per cent, you

*Some equations contain the possibility of a singular perturbation, where a big change happens in the results when a small change is given to the equation.

could change the instability point of that combination by a magnitude of 10! A 1,000 per cent change was big enough to make scientists rethink the way they looked at flow of multiple fluids through channels and pipes. Thanks to Rama and Balaji's work, a change in viscosity of the fluid had become a good way of understanding how to save on pumping energy.

Two months later, Balaji went back to IIT-M. Rama, however, stuck to the project he had left behind. She worked on it for the next two years and developed a theory for how it could be used in future fluid experiments. Finally, the results were published in 2001.

When Rama was in the fifth standard, her science teacher told everyone in class that oil and water cannot mix. It was a scientific fact, she explained. The teacher decided to demonstrate it as an experiment. She pulled out a jar and poured in oil and water. Then she shook the jar and put it back on the table.

'See?' the teacher said, pointing at the jar. 'Water and oil are immiscible. This means that they do not mix.'

'But, miss,' said nine-year-old Rama, 'that looks mixed!'

Her classmates laughed. Though oil and water are transparent, the liquid in the teacher's jar was now white and opaque. This was because many tiny droplets of oil had dispersed into the water. The oil was not lying on top of the water as a layer.

'That is because I just mixed them. Wait till tomorrow for it to settle down. It will separate,' said the teacher. 'They do not mix when the water and oil are still.'

SCIENCE SPEAK

THE TAO OF FLOW

Fluids flow in several ways – laminar, turbulent or something in-between. Go to your bathroom and open the water tap slowly. Observe how water flows in a thin, smooth line, like silk. This is called laminar flow. Now open the water tap to its full capacity. The water flow does not look smooth now. It becomes rough and choppy. This is called turbulent flow. Try this out with another fluid. Pour honey into a bowl slowly. It flows in a straight line. That's laminar flow.

There is always a point where a fluid turns from laminar flow to turbulent flow, called the laminar-turbulent transition. It's important to understand when this happens exactly so that it can be used to build efficient engines. Studying the movement of liquids and gases is essential to building rocket engines, wind turbines, oil pipelines and air conditioning systems.

INTERNS, STUDENTS AND SCIENTISTS

Every year, scientists like Rama receive requests from students who want to intern with them. Some are undergraduates who want to find out if they want to become scientists. They intern at various science institutions over their summer break. After staying on for a few months, and working on a project, they head back to their universities to complete their studies and courses.

Some students are doctoral (Ph.D) students, or scientists-in-the-making, who work on a single research topic. The topic could be anything from a small question about the human body (why does hair grow?) to big problems (how do black holes join together?).

A Ph.D student works with a scientist for five to six years, delving into a specific problem. The relationship between the doctoral student and the scientist who guides them (called their advisor) is important and mutually beneficial as each gives a lot to the other.

A scientist who is already established in their field of work can guide the Ph.D student on what kind of questions they should ask in their research. What is a good problem to work on? What should you look for? Advisors also pass on their ethics and ways of research to their students.

A student, on the other hand, comes with a new point of view, bringing a fresh energy to the unsolved problems of science. Together, the advisor and the student combine their energy, skills and experience to discover or invent brand new things.

A lot of Rama's research, for instance, has been sparked and aided by the students who worked with her like Balaji. Since she began her career, she has guided more than 100 students on various projects and is still in touch with most of them. 'I am proud of my students and interns. My research would not have been possible without them,' she says.

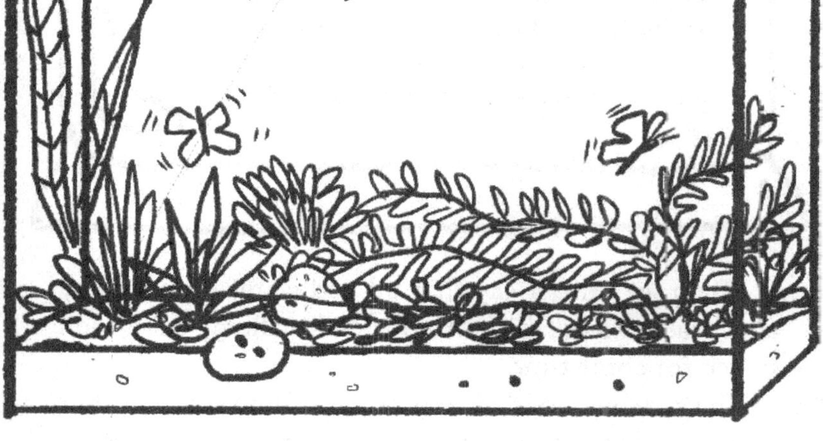

Foxy Facts

ALL ABOUT PLASMA

In physics, plasma has nothing to do with TV screens. Plasma is a state of matter. Have you been taught that there are three states of matter? Liquid, gas and solid? Nope! That isn't true. Plasma is the fourth state of matter. Plasma is fluid, like a liquid, but because of the charged particles present, it creates electromagnetic force.

'Then we cannot say that oil and water do not mix,' shot back Rama. 'When you shake them, they look mixed for some time.'

The teacher nodded and smiled, impressed by her bright student. It was on that day that Rama's interest

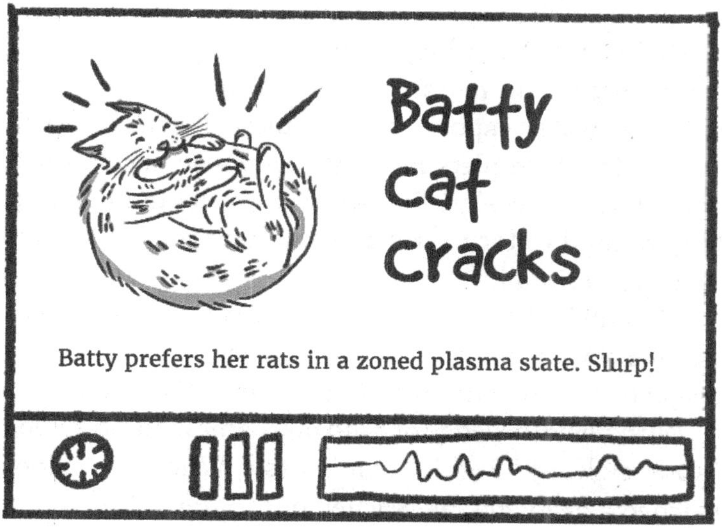

Batty prefers her rats in a zoned plasma state. Slurp!

in science was piqued. She wanted to observe the world around her and find logical answers to what was happening and why.

When Rama became a scientist, she found that the reason that the droplets of oil had dispersed in the water when her teacher shook the jar was turbulence. She began researching a field of physics called fluid mechanics, which explored the behaviour of fluids, like liquids and gases, in rest and in motion.

In 2013, when a student named Ravichandran Sivaramakrishnan (or Croor, as his classmates called him) came to her with the idea of researching the physics of cloud formation, she was thrilled. Rama had wanted to do this research to understand clouds from the point of view of physics for years.

Croor and Rama began by discussing and defining what they would research. 'A cloud is a group of tiny droplets, water vapour and turbulence,' said Rama to Croor. 'These droplets need turbulence to become rain and fall from the sky.' The two researchers decided that they wanted to formulate an equation for when clouds turned to rainfall.

'We will look at a cloud that is already formed, focus on one vortex in it, and try to answer how quickly droplets become raindrops in it,' Rama told Croor.

With her knowledge of fluid mechanics, Rama guided Croor skilfully. But it wasn't easy. Whenever Croor reached a dead end, he reached out to Rama for advice.

I am a scientist who shoots electricity in nanotubes. What is my name and in which chapter do I appear?

____

____

FOXY FACTS

WOODPECKERS, MIGRAINES AND FARTS

Here is a list of some weird research topics that people have spent a whole lot of time on:

- Do we fart for self-defence?
- Do cabbies have bigger brains?
- Which can jump higher, the dog flea or the cat flea?
- Why is wet underwear uncomfortable for us?
- Do woodpeckers get headaches?
- Do bees have a sweet tooth?
- Is cat food yummy for 12-year-olds?

What are the questions you would like to ask if you were doing a Ph.D?

____

____

____

They would then sit together and work on a solution to the problem. Between 2014 and 2017, they published five papers exploring water droplets in clouds.

By the time Croor completed his Ph.D, they had found a few answers. Through mathematical equations, they could prove that tiny droplets clustered and collided with each other near a vortex. This caused them to join together. A group of droplets thus became a raindrop, and that is one reason why rain occurred.

For her work, Rama was awarded the Shanti Swarup Bhatnagar Award. She now works as a professor at the Tata Institute of Fundamental Research in Bengaluru and continues to guide passionate Ph.D students. Currently, Rama is working on figuring out the physics of flows in the ocean. What is the physics behind waves? How does river water, when it reaches the ocean, affect the way the ocean behaves? These are some of the weighty questions that Rama is trying to answer through physics.

How Heat Blows up Balloons

Like water, air is also a fluid, though you can't see it. Do this experiment to see how air flow can blow up a balloon. Stretch a rubber balloon over the neck of an empty bottle. Put the bottle in hot water, or light a candle and hold the bottle over the flame. You will soon see that the balloon blows up.

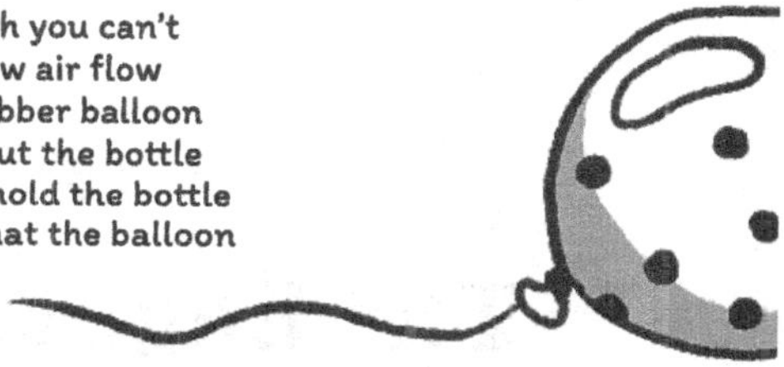

Explanation: When heat is added, the molecules of air in the bottle move faster and farther apart and therefore the gas (air) occupies more space. As more and more air flows into the balloon from the bottle, the walls of the elastic balloon are pushed out by the air. Heat causes the air to expand. What do you think will happen when you remove the heat? Try it. Now you know why it is necessary to check car tyres during hot weather.

This experiment was taken from a popular science website – ArvindGuptaToys.com – which teaches science principles through experiments. For more experiments like this, check out the website www.arvindguptatoys.com.

10

The Engine of the Oldest Molecule

It was a cold, winter evening in December 2009. The sun had set early, and darkness had engulfed the city of Stockholm in Sweden. Venkatraman Ramakrishnan, or Venki, as his friends and colleagues called him, hurried to the main entrance of the Stockholm Concert Hall. The biologist was dressed in formal attire: a white bow tie, crisp white shirt, a low-cut white waistcoat, a black tailcoat with silk facings, black trousers and shoes.

He entered the concert hall and was accompanied by an escort up the stage. He sat down in a velvet chair, which was in the front row of the carpeted stage. Across the stage sat members of Sweden's royal family and the members of the Nobel Committee*. The Royal Stockholm Philharmonic Orchestra played in a gallery above the stage.

*The Nobel Committee is a group of scientists and people responsible for selecting Nobel Prize winners.

FOXY FACTS

THE NOBLE NOBEL STORY

On 27 November 1895, Alfred Nobel, a Swedish scientist, inventor, entrepreneur and philanthropist signed his last will and testament, donating a large share of his fortune to create a series of prizes. Called the Nobel Prize, these awards would recognize outstanding contributions in physics, chemistry, physiology or medicine, literature and peace. To this day, the Nobel remains the most sought-after prize for sciences in the world.

Between 1901 and 2020, the Nobel Prize has been awarded 603 times to 934 men and women and 28 organizations to honour academic, cultural and scientific achievements. Recipients of the prize are called laureates. Only 57 of the total awardees are women. Malala Yousafzai from Pakistan, who shared the Nobel Peace Prize in 2014 with Kailash Satyarthi from India, was the youngest awardee ever. She was just 17 years old when she received the prize.

There have been six married couples who have been awarded the Nobel Prize. The latest one in 2019 went to Esther Duflow and Abhijit Banerjee, who shared the Nobel Prize in Economic Sciences with Michael Kremer for their experimental approach to alleviating global poverty. Besides Abhijit and Venki, eight Indian and Indian-origin stalwarts have received the Nobel Prize. Can you find out who they are and fill in the names below?

	NAME	YEAR	FIELD
1			
2			
3			
4			
5			
6			
7			
8			

Behind him, in neat rows of velvet chairs, sat some of the most illustrious scientists in the world. It was a big night for all of them.

The award ceremony started with an introductory speech. Soon, Venki's name was called out. He got up and greeted the king of Sweden, His Majesty Carl XVI Gustaf. He came back to his chair, gripping the velvet box that he had just received. Inside it was a gold coin. This coin was considered the highest prize in science – the Nobel Prize.

There was just one thought in his head – how thankful he was that he had stubbornly kept working on a small molecule called the ribosome.

Venki was born in 1952 in Chidambaram, a temple town in Tamil Nadu. When he was three years old, his family moved to Baroda in Gujarat, where his father started the biochemistry department at the University of Baroda. His parents were both scientists and worked together. Venki would often visit their laboratory and help out by putting crushed ice in the centrifuge so that the samples inside remained cold. He also hung out with his parents' scientist friends who visited their home from all around the world.

As a child, he decided that he liked the life of a scientist. He wanted to become one when he grew up. The opportunity came when Venky received a scholarship to Ohio University in the USA to do a Ph.D in physics. Little did he know that he was about to face a huge setback. Within a year of joining the doctoral program at Ohio, he realized he liked *biology* better than physics!

'It's a lot of theory and not enough experimentation,' he told his friend. Venki read up on advances in biology and life sciences in the journal *Scientific American*. Could he use his knowledge of physics on biology experiments, he wondered. These thoughts were pushed away when he met and married Vera Rosenberry in 1975. He also obtained his Ph.D in physics in 1976, a month before their first child was born. By this time, he was pretty sure he was in the wrong spectrum of science.

'Biology is undergoing a dramatic transformation,' he told Vera. 'I'm particularly interested in molecular biology – it's reporting a major breakthrough every month!'

Vera supported her husband's decision to do another doctorate in biology at the University of California in the USA. It was tough. He had to learn laboratory work and understand genetics, biochemistry and cell biology, all of which were new to him.

One day, when he was reading his favourite journal, *Scientific American*, he came across a research paper from Yale University about scientists who were working on ribosomes (See page 124). They were using a new methodology to explore the molecule. It was called neutron scattering, a technique which physicists used but biologists normally didn't.

'This is it!' he exclaimed. Venki read the study and connected with one of the authors of the study, Peter Moore. Peter offered him a position in Yale's ribosome project to do postdoctoral research.

'Hasn't the problem been solved already?' asked one of his friends. There were scientists already working on ribosomes, and antibiotics had been developed that stopped its work in spreading bacteria in the human body. The friend thought Venki was wasting his time

HORRIBLE HAIKU

Immensely intricate
A tiny ribosome dances
On the stunned
scientist

on something that had already been done. 'You should work on a relevant problem,' he added.

'If everyone does that, our understanding of the phenomena will be quite superficial,' Venki replied. He looked at a ribosome like a car. Scientists knew it had four wheels and windows and a driver. They did not know how it worked, what made it move or what its engine was made of. He wanted to understand the ribosome's engine.

In 1978, Venki moved to New Haven to do postdoctoral research in ribosomes. 'This is going to be hard,' Peter warned him on his first day at the lab. Ribosomes were complicated structures and decoding them was a fundamental problem to solve in biology. 'Even if I chip away at the problem, it will be useful,' replied Venki.

He got down to work and learnt a technique called small-angle neutron scattering*, used in research laboratories to explore the nature of materials. Venki would have to use this technique to understand the basic structural features of the ribosome and its components. Venki realized quickly how difficult the task was going to be.

*Neutrons are electrically neutral subatomic particles present in the nucleus of atoms. Neutron scattering is a method by which scientists cause tiny nuclear reactions in atoms of a material to study neutrons.

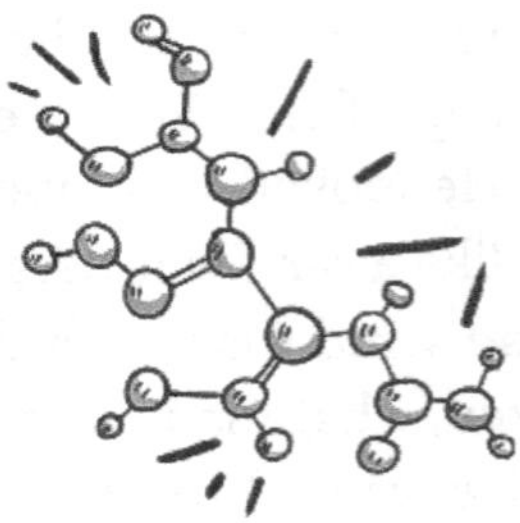

SCIENCE SPEAK

WHAT IS A RIBOSOME?

All matter, from humans to rocks to snails and moss, is made up of cells. These are made up of molecules, which are made up of groups of atoms.

A ribosome is a molecule that produces proteins. Making proteins is hugely important work as they carry out all the functions of life. Proteins make the muscles in the body move, let us sense light, touch and heat, and help us fight off disease.

Miniscule protein-making powerhouses, ribosomes play a crucial role in the game of life. Every cell in every form of life is either made by ribosomes or by enzymes that are made by them. Millions of life forms exist because ribosomes make proteins for them. As you read this, ribosomes in each of the trillions of cells in your body will have churned out thousands of proteins, so you can keep going.

Even measuring a small signal from a protein took several days. He patiently began collecting data, taking breaks and then heading to the beach with his family to unwind.

In 1983, Venki took up a new job at the Brookhaven National Laboratory in New York. Here, he continued to study ribosomes using the neutron scattering technique. He kept at it for years. But progress was frustratingly slow. In 1985, Venki met Steve White, a colleague who had previously worked in a laboratory in Berlin. Steve told him about a new technique that could be used for ribosome research called crystallography. Venki had heard a lecture on it by Ada Yonath, another Berlin-based scientist doing ribosomal research.

To use this technique, Venki had to learn how to make protein crystals so that he could study them. Making these was tedious work. He had to mix one drop of protein solution with a small amount of alcohol. The drop was placed on a thin glass slide and inverted. The protein drop fell slowly and crystallized. He failed many times. But a few months later, he had managed to make crystals of a ribosomal protein called S5.

Now that Venki had the S5 crystals, he wanted to learn X-ray crystallography, a new way with which he could look at ribosomes. At that time, the best lab doing crystallography was the MRC Laboratory of Molecular Biology (LMB lab) in Cambridge, UK. In 1991, Venki moved to Cambridge and started to work on ribosomes using crystallography.

Though the new technique was difficult, it yielded better results. Soon he had made a detailed map of the S5.

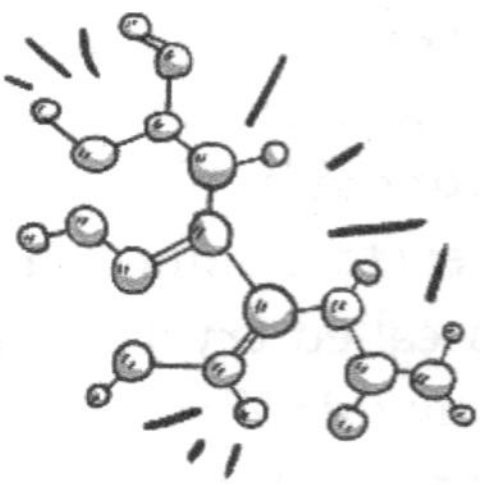

SCIENCE SPEAK

HOW TINY IS THE RIBOSOME?

Imagine you're an alien on Mars looking down at Earth. It's really, really far away. If you squint your many eyes, you can observe tiny objects moving around on the surface of the planet. If you are able to get a little closer, you might see that these objects move only when even smaller objects enter them and stop moving when they step out of them.

But you have absolutely no idea what these objects really are or how they work. You are simply unaware that animals and humans live and walk on Earth.

For a structural biologist like Venki, looking through a microscope at a ribosome molecule is a similar experience. It's an enormous and complex world in itself. You can observe some parts of it, but you can't figure out what these tiny dots do or how they work.

It was a beautiful moment! 'The curtains of the black box have parted,' he said as soon as he had completed the structure of the S5 protein.

In 1995, Venki worked on a new part of the ribosome – the protein 30S. But even after working on it for a year, he did not have crystals of the protein. At a conference in Europe, he found out that Ada had already made crystals of 30S. Suddenly, he was anxious. He called Richard Henderson, the director at the LMB lab and his mentor.

'What if it takes me years to get results?' he asked.

'Keep at it. You have a good chance of solving it,' Richard answered, encouraging him.

Venki followed Richard's advice and decided to work obsessively to uncover the structure of the 30S. He was finally successful, and his team developed maps of it.

Dr Nobel, Batty demands a rat-cloning machine to satiate Batty's hunger.

Much to their surprise, they discovered that they had managed to identify seven proteins in the 30S maps!

'This is a bigger breakthrough than I had imagined,' said Venki.

'It is as exciting as eating potato chips!' his colleague quipped.

Though the results were great for Venki and his collaborators, biochemists around the world were not too pleased when they realized that they would have to change the way they were looking at the ribosome protein. What Venki had discovered had changed how the ribosome would be studied forever.

Within a year, Venki was working towards creating detailed maps of of the 30S proteins when he saw another one of Ada's presentations at a conference. He noticed that she had made quite a lot of headway in her work as well. They were still in the race of who would get the results first!

'We have to solve this now!' Venki said as soon as he was back in his lab. Everyone worked on the proteins for 48 hours straight, without sleep, to make more crystals to be studied.

Once the crystals were ready, Venki travelled to Chicago's Structural Biology Center. He wanted to try out their crystallography machine. As the crystals ran through the machine, photographs came pouring into the computer. At the same lab, Venki and his team started to process it.

It was an exhaustive 48 hours of work. Disappointed, he saw that there was no result. His heart sank. This make-or-break trip was a failure. After a coffee break, he came back to the results again and realized he had made a mistake.

'We're going to be famous!' Venki cried out, starting to dance. A few days later, he returned to Cambridge, armed with detailed maps of the smallest of the 30S proteins, one of the proteins he found earlier. But the work was far from done.

'Pictures of complicated molecules look like a messy tangle of coloured pasta,' he said. 'We have to highlight their essential features.'

The 30S structure was complex. For months after, Venki worked on writing a scientific paper that would explain the results clearly. He also elaborated on how the ribosome worked and how antibiotics would block it.

It wasn't easy, but he finally published a paper. The scientific community was astounded by the results. He understood how the engine ran!

After Venki received the Nobel Prize, his days were busier. The month after he won the award was one long party. Venki attended one press conference after another, gave interviews, sat in banquets and conferences and gave lectures. When he got back to his lab in Cambridge, he was raring to get back to work. He did not want to lose steam and get distracted from his research after winning the Nobel.

By January 2010, he was working on unravelling the secrets of the ribosome. He now worked with the latest technique – an electron microscope – to decode ribosomes further. With new technology, the results were quicker, more detailed and accurate.

'It's ironic that now it will take only a week or two to get the structure of a ribosome,' he said, shaking his head as he looked at the ribosome molecule through an electron microscope. Using this technology, he and his colleagues found that there was much more to be explored in the invisible ribosome.

'When we have a clear goal in mind, we think we are struggling to reach a summit. But there is no summit,' he said in a lecture. 'When we get there, we realize we have just climbed a foothill, and there is an endless series of mountains ahead, waiting to be climbed.' For his contribution to science as a person of Indian origin, Venki was awarded the Padma Vibhushan by the government of India. In 2015, he was elected to serve a five-year term as president of the Royal Society of London, a big honour in science circles.

Venki, meanwhile, is back at his laboratory, exploring ribosomes. 'It will be a difficult problem for quite a while,' he says. There are still endless mountains to scale before humans figure out the tiny molecule called the ribosome!

The biographical information in this chapter has been acquired with permission from Venki Ramakrishnan's remarkable biography on his work and life, Gene Machine: The Race to Decipher the Secrets of the Ribosome.

Grow Your own Crystals

Making protein crystals, like Venki did for his experiments, is hard to do. However, making crystals of other materials in chemistry is not terribly complicated. Here's how you can make crystals with sugar. You can also try this process with salt.

Method

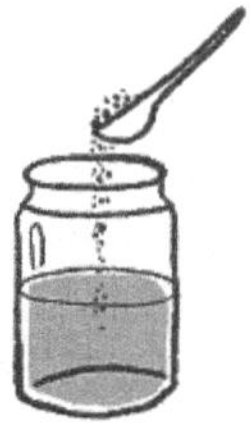

1 Take distilled drinking water. Boil it in a pan.

2 Mix three times the sugar into the water. Keep mixing the sugar until it completely dissolves.

3 Fill a tall jar with this solution.

4 Cut a piece of string with scissors and tie it to a pencil.

5 Put the string into the jar so that it is in two inches inside the solution.

6 Place the pencil across the opening of the jar so the thread hangs inside.

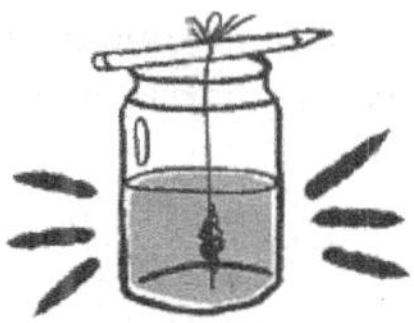

7 Let the mixture cool slowly.

8 Leave the experiment and wait for sugar crystals to form along the string.

Draw out how the crystals look in a day, a week and two weeks. How is it different?

One Day	One WEEK	TWO WEEKS

Take the crystals to your laboratory in school. Look at them under a microscope. Can you see any microorganisms on the crystals? Note down the results.

Answers

1. A Sixty-Million-Year-Old Frog

Sleuth Snoop, Page 12: Divya Mudappa

2. A New Way to Scatter Light

Sleuth Snoop, Page 28: Dr Venkatraman Ramakrishnan. He found the structure of the ribosome.

3. A Drug to Reverse Memory Loss

Sleuth Snoop, Page 40: Dr Vidita Vaidya, A Way to Decode the Brain

Colour Your Brain, Page 43: 1. Frontal Lobe 2. Parietal Lobe 3. Occipital Lobe 4. Cerebellum 5. Brain Stem 6. Temporal Lobe

4. A Protein That Smashes Cancer Cells

Sleuth Snoop, Page 52: Dr Venkatraman Ramakrishnan. The Engine of the Oldest Molecule

Mind Blowing Accidental Discoveries, Page 57: A-3, B-4, C-5, D-1, E-2

5. An Automatic Way to Do Mathematics

Sleuth Snoop, Page 67: Rama Govindarajan

6. A Way to Decode the Brain

Sleuth Snoop, Page 74: Like Vidita, Vijayalakshmi is a neuroscientist who studies the human brain. She also uses mice in her laboratory. (Please don't tell Batty.)

The Brainy Quiz: 1. True 2. False 3. True 4. False 5. True 6. True 7. True 8. True 9. True 10. False 11. True 12. False 13. True 14. True 15. False

7. A Hammer to Break a Cell Wall

Sleuth Snoop, Page 86: Sanjeev Das, Biochemistry

8. A New Field of Science

It's All in Your Genes, Page 95: 1-F, 2-G, 3-D, 4-C, 5-A, 6-E, 7-B

Sleuth Snoop, Page 95: Manjula Reddy, A Hammer to Break a Cell Wall

9. An Equation for Monsoon Clouds

Sleuth Snoop, Page 114: Ajay Sood, Electricity in Invisible Tubes

10. The Engine of the Oldest Molecule

The Noble Nobel Story, Page 120

Rabindranath Tagore 1913 Literature

CV Raman 1930 Physics

Har Gobind Khorana 1968 Physiology/Medicine

Mother Teresa 1979 Peace

Subramanyan Chandrasekhar 1983 Physics

Amartya Sen 1998 Economic Sciences

VS Naipaul 2001 Literature

Kailash Satyarthi 2014 Peace

CV Raman

Manindra Agrawal

Manjula Reddy

Vidita Vaidya

Sanjeev Das

Copyright Acknowledgements

Copyright Acknowledgements

Photograph of JC Bose: public domain
Photograph of Divya Mudappa by TR Shankar Raman/NCF
Photograph of Anil Bhardwaj: Infosys Science Foundation

Archana Sharma

JC Bose

Amit Agrawal

Anil Bhardwaj

Ajay Sood

Divya Mudappa

Answers

1. The World's Largest Ice Stupa

Sleuth Snoop, Page 11: Divya Mudappa, a rainforest

2. An Electronic Dog to Sniff Out Bombs

Sleuth Snoop, Page 25: Ayyappanpillai Ajayaghosh

3. A Rainforest in the Middle of a Tea Estate

Sleuth Snoop, Page 39: Kartik Shanker

Spot and Colour All 15 Animals, Page 45 →

4. A Rocket to Poke Martians

Sleuth Snoop, Page 69: An Electronic Dog to Sniff Out Bombs

Match the Spacecraft, Page 74: 1-E, 2-D, 3-A, 4-F, 5-C, 6-B

I Spy with a Telescope, Page 75: ACROSS: 4 Asteroid, 5 Star, 6 Meteor

DOWN: 1 Satellite, 2 Galaxy, 3 Comet

5. A Machine to Annoy Plants

Sleuth Snoop, Page 83: CERN, Archana Sharma

6. An All-Seeing Electronic Eye

Sleuth Snoop, Page 93: Blood Plasma Separation Microdevice

The Ultimate Science Crossword, Page 98: ACROSS: 4 Research, 6 Patent, 7 Thesis

DOWN: 1 Scientist, 2 Nobel, 3 Journal, 5 Data

7. A Camera for Subatomic Particles

Sleuth Snoop, Page 105: Payload, Anil Bhardwaj

8. Self-Growing Molecular Materials

Sleuth Snoop, Page 126: Ramgopal Rao, An Electronic Dog to Sniff Out Bombs

Colour Me Chemical, Page 129:

1 Gas bottle	2 Evaporating dish	3 Mortar and pestle
4 Iron ring	5 Crucible and cover	6 Wire gauze
7 Test tube rack	8 Test tube	9 Beaker
10 Dropper	11 Wire brush	12 Forceps
13 Tongs	14 Funnel	15 Micropipets
16 Spatula	17 Buret	18 Utility Clamp
19 Ring stand	20 Watch glass	21 24-well plate
22 Wash bottle	23 Safety goggles	24 Pipet
25 Erlenmeyer flask	26 Corks	27 Bunsen Burner
28 Thermometer	29 Graduated cylinder	30 Test tube holder

9. A Microdevice to Split Blood

Sleuth Snoop, Page 132: Rama Govindarajan

Which Simple Machines Do I Use? Page 139: 1B Ramp, 2D Faucet, 3E Elevator, 4A Nail Clipper, 5F Scissors, 6C Bottlecap

Invent: A Magic Magnet

You'll Need:

A long iron nail
A magnet
A safety pin

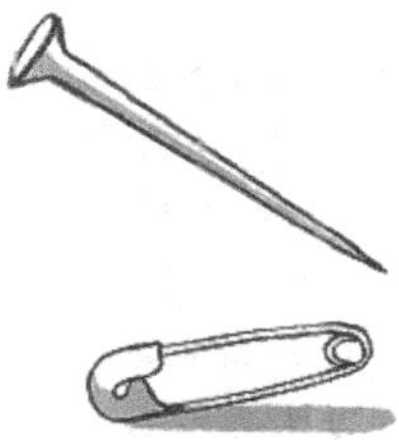

1 Show your audience that the iron nail is not magnetic by trying to pull a safety pin up with it.

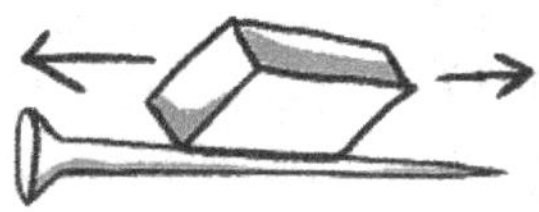

2 Now, rub the iron nail with your real magnet. Make the same movement from top to bottom, repeating it 30-40 times. Mutter a spell for the benefit of your audience while you do this.

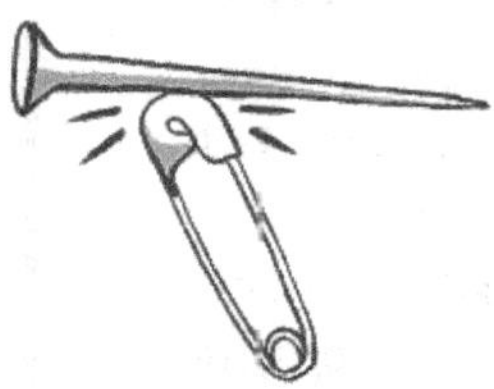

3 Touch the iron nail to the safety pin. Your audience will clap as you are able to pull the safety pin up with your newly minted magnet.

Think about why something happens. Why do you *think* the fan moves when you switch it on? List down all your theories. Does a pigeon sit inside it and push the fan blade? Is it magic? Does some invisible energy push the blade? Don't discard any of your guesses yet. These guesses are your hypotheses.

4. **Test your hypothesis by conducting an experiment.** Set up an experiment, or a test, to check if your prediction is accurate. Observe the fan. Can you see a pigeon pulling the blades? No. So that's not a potential answer. What is the switch attached to? A wire. What does the wire have? Test the wire. Is it electricity that moves the fan?
5. **Communicate your results:** Tell your classmates and your teacher about your result. Does the conclusion you have drawn make sense to everyone? Does it seem like the right reason for the fan to move? If they agree on the results, get them published in the school paper.
6. **Congratulations, you are now a scientist!**

First published in 2021 by Hachette India
(Registered name: Hachette Book Publishing India Pvt. Ltd)
An Hachette UK company
www.hachetteindia.com

SRD

Page 134 is an extension of this copyright page.

ISBN 978-93-89253-97-9

Hachette Book Publishing India Pvt. Ltd
4th & 5th Floors, Corporate Centre
Plot No. 94, Sector 44, Gurugram – 122003, India

Typeset in Chaparral Pro 12/14.8
by Manmohan Kumar, Delhi

Printed and bound in India by
Manipal Technologies Limited, Manipal

MIX
Paper from responsible sources
FSC™ C043100

SHWETA TANEJA

THEY FOUND WHAT?

STORIES OF DARING DISCOVERIES BY INDIAN SCIENTISTS

ILLUSTRATIONS BY
SHARANYA KUNNATH

hachette INDIA

SHWETA TANEJA

THEY MADE WHAT?

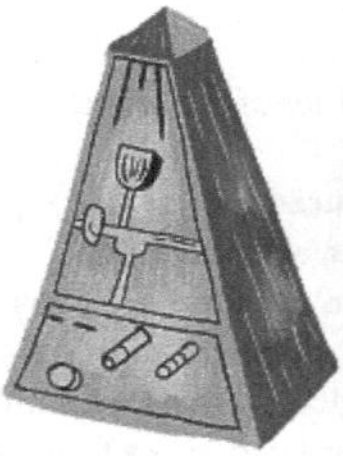

STORIES OF INGENIOUS INVENTIONS BY INDIAN SCIENTISTS

ILLUSTRATIONS BY
SHARANYA KUNNATH

hachette INDIA

First published in 2021 by Hachette India
(Registered name: Hachette Book Publishing India Pvt. Ltd)
An Hachette UK company
www.hachetteindia.com

SRD

ISBN 978-93-89253-97-9

Hachette Book Publishing India Pvt. Ltd
4th & 5th Floors, Corporate Centre
Plot No. 94, Sector 44, Gurugram – 122003, India

Typeset in Chaparral Pro 12/14.8
by Manmohan Kumar, Delhi

Printed and bound in India by
Manipal Technologies Limited, Manipal

Shweta Taneja writes fiction and science for kids and adults. Her writing has given her many global accolades. She was a finalist in the prestigious French award Grand Prix de l'Imaginaire (2020), awarded the Charles Wallace Writing Fellowship (2016) and has given talks at WorldCon (2019), Eurocon (2018) and the Cartoon Museum London (2016).

However, her most cherished award remains a painting of an owl (nicknamed Speky) gifted by an 11-year-old fan. Speky, along with Batty and Foxy remind her every day to laugh, work hard and create fascinating worlds for her readers. Join her for tea and conversations on creatures and writing through her handle @shwetawrites or email her at me@shwetawrites.com.

Contents

1

The World's Largest Ice Stupa

It was dark and cold outside. Freezing winds swooshed from one side of the high mountains to the other, whistling frozen songs. Uleptokpo, a tiny village in Ladakh, India's northern-most union territory, consisted of five huddled houses. In one of the houses, a warm fire burned in a fireplace, in the middle of the kitchen. Around it sat seven-year-old Sonam Wangchuk, with his three older brothers and their mother. They were quiet, rapturously listening to their grandmother tell a story.

It was Granny's favourite story, about a lady who wanted a sip of water in the deep of winter – but there was no water to be found. So she brought Father Glacier from one valley and Mother Glacier from the other. She put them together under the boulders and that was how Baby Glacier was formed. When Baby Glacier grew, it provided water to the lady and the people of the land.

'Glaciers can't have babies!' scoffed Sonam. 'They're made of ice!'

His mother laughed. 'It's a story, Sonam. It tells us how the Ladakhi people knew about glacier grafting.'

'What's glacier grafting?' he asked.

'The art of creating artificial glaciers,' she replied.

'Wait, what? Glaciers can be created by people?' exclaimed Sonam. 'Then why don't we make some? We can solve our water problem, and I can wash the dishes properly.'

Everybody burst out laughing. Sonam slipped into a thoughtful mood. He knew water would solve a lot of problems for his village.

Towering at a height of 3,100 metres above sea level, Uleptokpo, Sonam's village, sits in the middle of Ladakh, the world's highest desert.

Water shortages were a constant in Uleptokpo, which depended on two sources of water. In the spring, the snow would melt and provide water called snowmelt. In the summer, the glaciers would melt and give them water called glacier melt. During the springtime planting season, they would face a drought. During the summer, when the sharp sun shone and the glaciers melted too soon, his village would be flooded for a month.

Sonam was the youngest in his family. He lived with his parents, grandmother and brothers. His brothers helped their mother clear the snow during winter. In spring and summer, they helped out on the farm. His family grew barley, wheat, vegetables, cabbage, cauliflower,

spinach, and fruits like apricots, pears, walnuts and apples. But in any season, Sonam was responsible for washing the dishes.

He hated washing dishes! The reason was simple – washing required water, which was always in short supply in his village. During winter, when temperatures dipped to -20° Celsius, Sonam and his brothers would trek for one kilometre to a frozen stream with a pick and a jerry can. They would break the ice, make a hole and dip the cans in to fill water. Then, they would lug the cans back home. Sonam would wash the dishes indoors. The water was icy cold, and his fingers would turn blue and numb.

If it was spring or summer, Sonam would put all the unwashed dishes into a bucket and take them down to the stream. The water, which consisted of melted ice from a nearby glacier, was *still* icy cold! In the high summer, the water in the stream would evaporate and was barely there. No wonder Sonam was so interested in getting a steady supply of water to his village!

Uleptokpo had no school, and it was his grandmother and mother who were responsible for his schooling. Granny told him stories, and his mother helped him read and write in Ladakhi. From them, Sonam learnt how important it was to use locally available materials and recycle everything. 'Solutions to problems need to be simple,' his mother would tell him. Doing practical, day-to-day activities helped Sonam understand how the basic principles of science could be used to meet the needs of everyday life.

WOEFUL WATER

Ladakh is an arid region filled with spectacular mountains and vast blue skies. There are 200 villages scattered across this high-altitude desert. The climate is demanding. Winter temperatures dip below -20° Celsius, and there is less than four inches of precipitation (or snow and rain combined) all through the year.

The main occupation in rural Ladakh is farming. People in the villages rely on the glaciers frozen in the higher mountains above for water. With such a great dependence on nature, Ladakh has seen the effects of climate change much earlier than the big Indian cities. The snowline has shifted, and glaciers are receding. Glacial streams are drying out even before summer starts, creating extreme water scarcity during spring when saplings are vulnerable.

Though Ladakh has seen it first, water shortage will soon be a problem for all of India. If you have enough water for everyday use in your home, you are privileged. India has more than 1.3 billion people, half of whom do not have access to adequate water.

Scientists say that by the year 2100, 70 to 99 per cent of the glaciers in the Hindu Kush-Himalayan region* will be gone. How old will you be then? What will you do if you do not have enough water?

*The Hindu-Kush Himalayas are a major source of freshwater for South Asia and some parts of Southeast Asia. Water originating from this 800-kilometre-long stretch of the Himalayas (through melted snow, glaciers and rainfall) feeds the largest river systems in Asia.

'Can't we make our own glacier?' he asked his mother one day, thinking on her advice.

'We have lost the art of glacier grafting,' she said.

Sonam's mind became obsessed with creating glaciers.

When he turned nine, his father enrolled him in a school in Srinagar. But Sonam struggled to fit in as he couldn't speak any of the languages his schoolmates spoke. He was lonely and acted up – his teachers thought of him as a rebel and punished him. 'I don't like studying here,' he told his father. Sonam wanted to join his brothers at their school in New Delhi. But his father was adamant that he stay at his Srinagar school.

When he was 12 years old, Sonam ran away from school. He took a bus heading to Jammu and changed three more buses to reach the Vishesh Kendriya Vidyalaya, a government school for kids from India's border regions, in Delhi, where his brothers were studying. He walked into the principal's office and asked to be admitted.

'I want to study here,' he told the shocked principal, who rang up his father and admitted him into the school. Surrounded by his brothers and kind teachers, Sonam began to enjoy studying. He found that he was especially good at science and loved thinking of ideas to invent things. One of them was definitely a glacier!

'Before you invent something, you need to find a problem that needs a solution,' his science teacher told him. This statement got Sonam thinking. He also remembered how his mother told him that solutions needed to be simple. He had an idea! Sonam wanted

to wake up at 3 a.m. in the morning to study, but he would keep sleeping through the alarm. So he decided to invent something that could wake him up early.

His science teacher had just started teaching the class about the functions of a pulley. He decided to use this mechanism to build an alarm system. Sonam hung an alarm clock from the ceiling with a string. The clock was attached to a big mug filled with water. If the alarm rang for more than 30 seconds, it would tilt, the mug would upturn and splash cold water on Sonam's face! He soon started to wake up at 3 a.m. as planned.

Sonam's next invention was equally interesting. Delhi had terribly hot summers, and the heat turned his room into an oven. So, he created a natural air-conditioning system to keep it cool using a double bed sheet to make a cubicle in the corner of his room, leaving a gap of a few inches from the floor. A jug filled with water hung with a pulley system above this sheet. When he pulled the rope, a small pipe would send water up and drip it onto the sheet, making it wet. As evaporation cooled the air in the cubicle, the cool air would sink down and escape from the gap near the floor. His handmade air conditioner brought the temperature down by 7–8 degrees!

When he finished his engineering degree, Sonam decided to become a teacher. In 1988, he moved to Leh and started the Students Educational and Cultural Movement of Ladakh (SECMOL). The alternative school was set up with the aim of teaching students to find

solutions to the unique problems of mountain people. For the first few years, he worked with government schools across Ladakh to understand and change the way children were taught.

During his research, he found that one of the reasons Ladakhi kids hated school was because it was just too cold. In early winters, the temperature in schoolrooms dropped to -15° Celsius. How could they write exams when their hands were freezing?

'Ladakh has 300 sunny days every year,' Sonam told his brothers. 'Why can't we use the sun to heat our schools?' At this time, they were designing SECMOL's campus and had already finalized its location. The school would be situated in the village of Phey, 17 kilometres from Leh. 'We have to lead by example,' he said to himself.

Sonam decided to design the whole campus with solar heating and no electric heaters. He wanted to use natural materials, and began to research how he could construct a building that would remain warm, even when temperatures dropped to -25° Celsius. That's when he noticed the mud houses that the Ladakhi people had been building for thousands of years, with thicker walls to conserve the heat inside! He reengineered this indigenous design – the walls would be one foot thick, made of clay and straw, to trap the heat. He added south-facing windows and skylights, which let the sunlight in through the day. There were greenhouses attached to the south side, where the sun shone the most, which made sure the attached building stayed warm.

Batty cat cracks

Meowrr. Batty was a kitten when she invented her first scuttler-catching apparatus. What's the big deal? Batty's now working on inventing these machines:

Rato-scope: An infrared artificial eye to track a rat in a different neighbourhood.

Miceinator: A special mincing device to help prepare Batty's favourite lunch.

What are the machines you want to invent, my meows?

In 1999, the SECMOL campus was finally ready. It had 20 rooms and one large school building, all of which were solar-heated and environment-friendly. A low-cost solar heater provided hot water to the bathing blocks and solar cookers were used in the kitchen. The toilets were constructed in traditional Ladakhi style*. Sonam had also managed to design a low-cost greenhouse so

*Ladakhi toilets are an eight-by-eight-foot pit. You sit on a hole on top of the pit and do your routine. There is no flush. Human faeces collect in the pit below and turn into manure, which is used on farms. In SECMOL, it was used in the campus's vegetable garden and trees.

they had a thousand trees on campus – in the middle of a high-altitude desert!

For the next 20 years, Sonam worked hard to improve the quality of education in Ladakh. In 2008, he met actor Aamir Khan at an event in Mumbai. Aamir had seen a documentary on Sonam's work at SECMOL. Later, his movie *3 Idiots* went on to feature Sonam and his innovative inventions. The immensely popular character, Phunsukh Wangdu, played by Aamir Khan in the movie, was in fact inspired by Sonam. The inventor started to get calls from friends, strangers and people in the media.

'You're that character from *3 Idiots*!' the callers would say.

'No,' he would reply. 'I'm Sonam, not Phunsukh Wangdu.'

Because of the movie, Sonam and SECMOL were in the news. People from around the world flocked to the school and wanted to work there. Sonam was invited to dozens of conferences and workshops. He found this attention unwanted but decided to use it to spread his message on education.

At this time, climate change had begun to affect sensitive places like Ladakh. While people in the cities still led comfortable lives, mountain people were increasingly facing floods and droughts because of the adverse changes in the environment.

Since winters were shorter, villages began to face a water shortage in April and May, when there was not enough snowmelt to water their farms. This meant

that they would not be able to grow enough food for the winter. Because of global warming, the glaciers, on which the Ladakhi people depended, had receded as well. They had to trek higher up to get water even in the severe cold.

It is high time someone did something about this, thought Sonam. He remembered the story his grandmother had told him all those years ago. What if the Ladakhi people actually knew how to make artificial glaciers but had only forgotten the art? Could the ancient technique be revived, just like the mud houses?

He went to meet a well-known Ladakhi engineer he knew to have a conversation about it. Aba Chewang Norphel was known as the Ice Man of India. In 1986, he had created the first artificial glacier in Leh to solve the water problem for villages and farms nearby. To make a glacier, he had to dig a pit near an existing one. All through the winter, glacier melt would drip into this pit, freezing overnight in the sub-zero temperatures. Come spring, the ice would turn into water and become a stream for the villages nearby!

Aba had built dozens of these glaciers by 2009. But the artificial glacier design had problems. Under the sharp Ladakh sun, they melted by April, way before farmers needed water for their crops. To make sure they wouldn't melt too fast, these glaciers had to be made at a height of 4,000 metres and in the shade. But getting water from this height down to the villages, a thousand metres below, was a tough job.

'I can't make a glacier near the village. That's too low an altitude,' explained Aba.

'I don't want to climb all the way to the ice field to get water for my home,' said one of the women in the village. Sonam racked his brains – there had to be a solution to this conundrum. Was it possible to make a glacier at 3,000 metres? Sonam created a team with a few senior students at SECMOL to work on this project along with him.

'How can we make sure that a glacier melts slowly so that it lasts till May and June instead of melting in April? This is when the people in the villages need water the most,' he explained.

Sleuth Snoop

I spy another scientist in this book whose work helped combat climate emergency. Who am I talking about? What did they build?

____

____

'It's impossible,' said one student. 'It's May now. All the ice has melted around us.'

It was true. In May, at the start of the Ladakhi summer, all the ice and snow around them had already melted. Higher up in the mountains, they could still see ice, but there was none to be found around them. Sonam and his students put their heads together and came up with ideas, but none of them seemed workable.

Sonam decided to take a break one day and went for a ride on his bicycle. He pedalled fast as strong winds whipped his face. As he rode past a rivulet and started to cross a bridge, something glistened. He stopped to investigate. He got off his bicycle and went around the bend to the corner of the bridge. The river underneath sparkled and shone.

Under the bridge lay a big chunk of ice. Even though it was the middle of May, and peak summer at that, the ice had still not melted. 'Of course!' cried Sonam. 'It can stay frozen because it's not exposed to the sun!' Two crows fluttered, startled, and cawed disapprovingly as Sonam rushed to his bicycle and went back to the SECMOL campus. 'Shade!' he yelled to his confused students. 'Shade is how we can grow ice at 3,000 metres!'

It was such a simple idea that Sonam almost berated himself for not having thought about it earlier. His mind whirred with possibilities. Where could he develop a glacier that could be kept under the shade? If he had to solve the water problems of an entire village, he needed a big chunk of ice to last through the months

of May, June, July and August. It had to melt slowly and provide water for the farms.

Maybe he could cover the ice surface with a material like canvas. That would protect the ice from melting too soon. But Sonam wasn't keen on this idea as it would make his invention expensive. He prided himself on making simple, low-cost inventions.

One day, he was teaching geometry at school. 'So, here's the thing. Certain shapes have a minimum surface area for a given volume,' said Sonam. Suddenly he stopped writing on the board and turned around. 'Oh!' he said. His confused students looked up from their notebooks, frowning. They were used to their teacher's eccentricity. Sonam, meanwhile, waved his arms around and ran out of the class.

'A cone, a cone, a cone!' he declared to no one in particular, whooping with joy as he ran down the corridor. He went to his desk and started drawing. It was a simple idea – the kind he liked. A cone's surface area was much smaller than a rectangular patch.

'Direct sunlight needs surface area to melt ice,' he explained to the team of students who were helping him with the glacier project. 'If we can make the surface area smaller, the ice will melt at a slower rate.'

'A cone!' his student repeated, marvelling at the ingenuity of the idea.

'Yes, a cone-shaped glacier,' said Sonam, grinning.

It was a brilliantly different idea. A cone-shaped glacier could work as its surface would be less exposed to the sun. *Conical ice mounds*, he thought, scribbling furiously.

Your Daily Water Meter

Track how much water you and your family use in your daily life for a week.

Dates for the week of __________ to __________

ACTIVITY	ESTIMATED AMOUNT OF WATER USED (IN LITRES)	SUN	MON	TUE	WED	THUR	FRI	SAT	TOTAL NUMBER OF TIMES	YOUR TOTAL WEEKLY WATER USE (IN LITRES)
Washing face or hands	4									
Taking a shower	50									
Taking a bucket bath	30									
Brushing teeth (normal running water)	5									
Brushing teeth (water turned off)	1									
Flushing the toilet	15									
Cooking a meal	5									
Drinking water	5									
Washing dishes by hand	20									
Cleaning house	8									
Washing a load of laundry	20									
Watering plants	5									
Washing car (with bucket)	10									
									TOTAL	

'That looks like a stupa*,' said a student, peeking at Sonam's designs.

'You're right! We will call it an ice stupa!'

Building a cone-shaped glacier proved to be a huge challenge. They needed to be able to spray water down from a height during winter so it could freeze overnight. In 2013, they prepared a small model in a bucket on a wall and experimented with it. Every morning, the ice cone would melt during the day. The model did not work. They needed to try something else.

'Let's go bigger,' said Sonam. He began to design the prototype. One of his students, Tenzing Shara, who was a mountaineer and had spent time in glaciers, suggested a wild idea. 'Why don't we use bushy thorns, so that the water has a surface to freeze on?' he said. Sonam liked the idea and added this to the prototype they were planning.

In the winter of 2014–15, the prototype was ready. They connected a glacier with a mud pipe going downhill. Glacier melt would go down this pipe towards the SECMOL campus. The pipe ended above a pool of water, spouting into a fountain. As the water rose up in a spray and fell back on the cone-shaped thorny structure, it froze in the sub-zero air, forming a natural cone.

By the time winter ended in early 2015, the ice stupa was 20 feet tall – as high as a two-storeyed house! Everyone in SECMOL was betting on how long the

*A stupa is a mound-like structure which is worshipped in Buddhist traditions. Since Ladakh is a Buddhist area, you can see this structure all over the region, decorated with prayer flags.

Batty cat cracks

Mr Ice Maker, it's time to treat Batty to some crunchy frozen rodents. *Meow!*

stupa would last before it began to melt. Some teachers said March, while some students were more confident and said mid-April. Sonam said it would last till 1 May.

It was impossible, thought the students and teachers, as no one had seen a glacier last in the harsh sunlight of Ladakh for that long. Much to their surprise, the glacier lasted beyond their wildest hopes, till 18 May, and watered the plants and trees in the SECMOL campus!

During this time, Sonam had also contacted the Phyang Monastery nearby and showed them the ice stupa. They were impressed and asked Sonam to build one for the village of Phyang.

'I want to plant 5,000 trees around the new ice stupa in the village,' he told the head of Phyang Monastery. The stupa would provide water for the new saplings.

The head okayed the project, and Sonam started to crowdsource the money from across the world. By now, word had spread that a crazy engineer was building ice stupas in the world's highest desert!

Within a few months, Sonam was able to raise enough money to build the Phyang ice stupa. This was a bigger project than making the glacier at the campus. A pipe had to be laid for 2.3 kilometres, stretching from the glacier to the middle of the village. Curious village folk joined Sonam and his students, helping them plant 5,000 trees around the ice stupa!

The work ended by November 2015. Over the winters of 2015 and 2016, Phyang's ice stupa started to grow with glacier melt, bit by bit. In the spring of 2016, it was larger than the one in SECMOL campus. It was as high as a seven-floor apartment and became the largest ice stupa in the world! It also lasted way beyond summer – till the first week of August. It provided one million litres of water to the garden around it and helped grow a forest of 5,000 trees.

In 2018, Sonam and his students built more ice stupas in the upper valley of Phyang. Altogether, this meant 30 million litres of water for the villages below! Since then, the engineer, inventor and educationist has introduced his glacier-making technology to the government of Sikkim, and has even made these ingenious ice towers in Switzerland and Peru. Currently, the Ice Stupa Artificial Glacier Project has created 20 stupas across Ladakh that are 30 metres high, each capable of supplying 10 million litres of water to the villages around them.

FOXY FACTS

A TRIP TO THE SACRED STUPAS

Buddhism is widely practised by the people of Ladakh. In a clever tribute to Ladakhi culture, Sonam called his human-made glacier an ice 'stupa'. And so, they have become sacred sites for the Ladakhi people. In the summer of 2017, 12,000 visitors came to the Phyang ice stupa to pray. This works for the resourceful engineer. He knows that if it's a religious symbol, the people in the community are bound to take good care of it.

Sonam has been awarded the prestigious Rolex Award for Enterprise and the Ramon Magsaysay Award for his achievements in water conservation and glacier-making.

Sonam hopes that some of the students who helped him build the ice stupas will become entrepreneurs and build glaciers for a living. 'As climate change continues, artificial glaciers, unfortunately or fortunately, are the future,' he says. Sonam has many other plans up his sleeve for Ladakh, which a lot of people would find 'crazy'. One of them is to create a hotel made of ice, where tourists can stay during winters. This hotel will then melt and provide water to the villages in summer!

'Good innovations use minimum resources and make people's lives better,' he tells his students. Like his mother, he wants to use freely available materials like mud, sunlight, ice and water, and shape them into inventions that can solve the pressing problems of the mountain people.

Sunny Side up!

Sonam, as you may have figured out by now, likes simple designs. Many people ask him what his favourite solar energy gadget is. It's a clock that doesn't work! Called Campus Time, the clock in the SECMOL campus is one hour ahead of Indian Standard Time. This helps students go to bed early, get up early and take advantage of the sunlight as the sun rises at 5.30 a.m. Many people laugh when they hear this, calling Sonam eccentric. 'It's more eccentric to sleep through early morning sunlight and then use solar-powered batteries to light your nights,' he quips.

Can you create a simple solar energy gadget using household things? Research online and draw your design here:

2

An Electronic Dog to Sniff Out Bombs

It was Shiloh, a beagle, who gave Ramgopal Rao the idea for a bomb sniffer.

One day, he was sipping a cup of tea at home when he observed his daughter, Sneha, playing with Shiloh. Every time his daughter hid from Shiloh, the dog would find her quite easily.

'She's too smart,' complained Sneha. 'How does she know where I am every single time?'

'She's a beagle. They are known for their sense of smell,' said Sneha's mother.

Smell, thought Ramgopal, getting up from his chair, newspaper forgotten. Changing into his work clothes, he dashed off to his laboratory on the campus of the Indian Institute of Technology, Bombay (IIT-B), where he was a professor and researcher.

'We are going to make an electronic nose!' he announced to his students at the lab.

'An electronic *nose*?' exclaimed one of his students.

'Yes. It will have the same accuracy as a sniffer dog,' Ramgopal replied excitedly.

Ramgopal had been working on an unusual assignment for the last few months. It had all begun in 2008, when the principal scientific advisor to the Government of India, Dr Rajagopala Chidambaram, had come to visit the scientist with a special request.

The years 2007 and 2008 had been terrible for India. There had been a series of bomb blasts in public places across the country. In 2007, bombs had gone off twice in Hyderabad, once in a garden and once in a masjid. Explosions had also happened in a train in Haryana, in a movie theatre in Ludhiana, and in a Lucknow courthouse. In 2008, the spate of bomb explosions in public spaces continued. Hundreds of people lost their lives in terror attacks in Mumbai, Bengaluru and Delhi.

The government was concerned about the security of its citizens and wanted to make public spaces safe again. This was the intention with which Dr Chidambaram approached Ramgopal – he wanted to find a way to detect bombs that did not involve sniffer dogs*.

*Sniffer dogs, also called detection dogs, are specially trained to use their sense of smell to detect dangerous things like explosives, illegal drugs, wildlife, currency, blood or even electronics. Since a dog's nose is up to a million times more sensitive than a human nose, they are very useful in security operations, especially to seek out things that are hidden from the human eye.

Foxy Facts

HOW TO TRAIN A BOMB SQUAD DOG

Dogs have a strong sense of smell, but how do you teach them to sniff out bombs? Firstly, dogs don't smell the bomb; they smell specific chemicals that make it up – ingredients like commercial dynamite, TNT and RDX.

The dog trainer places these individual chemical ingredients into cans and intersperses them with cans containing other materials like chemicals, foods, drugs and powders. The dog is made to smell the cans. Every time it finds the can with one of the bomb particles instead of other random things, it is rewarded. The reward is the dog's favourite food – a nibble

of a peanut butter biscuit or a slurpy bone. In a couple of months, the dog figures out that finding the bomb particle will result in a yummy snack. That's a huge motivation!

The training also includes what the dog has to do once it finds the smell. The trainer does not want the sniffer dog to paw and scratch a suitcase that might have a bomb. That would be dangerous. So the dog is trained to sit down once it smells the bomb particles and then look up at its trainer for a bite of its favourite food. This way, the trainer can take the dog away from the dangerous discovery and send in a bomb disposal squad.

'They are expensive to train,' explained Dr Chidambaram to Ramgopal. He wanted the scientist to come up with a cheaper and quicker alternative.

The reason why the scientific advisor had approached Ramgopal was because of his reputation as an innovative scientist who could find unique solutions to difficult engineering problems.

Ramgopal had grown up in a village called Kollapur in Telangana. He was the first student from his village to become an engineer. But he didn't take up a job immediately. Instead, he went to IIT-B to do a postgraduate degree in electrical engineering, and then to Germany for his Ph.D, and *then* to the USA for his post-doctoral studies. There, he was introduced to nanoelectronics, a branch of science that involves building tiny devices that are so small, they can't be seen by the human eye!

Ramgopal studied nanodevices to understand them better. A few years later, he joined IIT-B as a professor. By this time, he had discovered that he was good at designing miniscule devices that could make life better for people.

Sleuth Snoop

I spy a chemist in this book who works with nanomaterials. What's their name?

____

FOXY FACTS
UNSEEN NANODEVICES

Ramgopal specializes in making devices and gadgets that are so small that they are the size of how much your fingernail grows in one minute! Can you see how much your fingernail has grown as you were reading this? That is the size of a nanodevice.

A nanometre is a billionth of a metre. Nanotechnology is a branch of technology that deals with dimensions of less than 100 nanometres, creating miniscule gadgets called nanodevices that can change individual atoms and molecules. Nanodevices include nanosensors that can 'sense' a molecule, nanocameras that can take pictures of the insides of a cell, and nanochips that function as a whole computer. Being super-tiny, these devices are expensive to make. Human hands cannot make them. Specialized equipment and machines are used to create these devices.

Batty cat cracks

Purrr... Dr Nano, Batty wants a sniffer to sniff out devilish dogs and scurry them away.

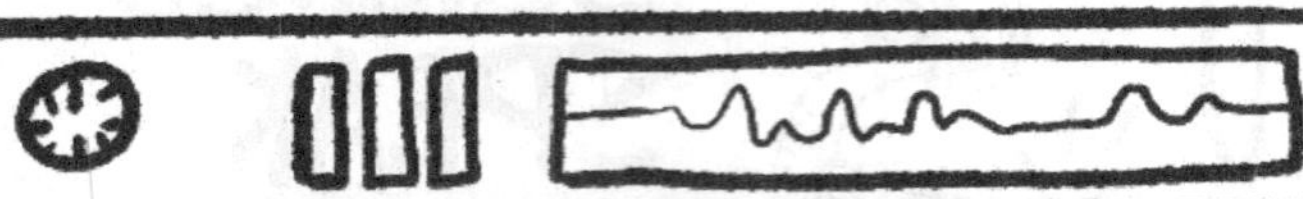

The first project he worked on aimed to improve the battery life of a phone. If he could reduce the energy usage of a device, it would save energy, which in turn would be good for the environment. It would also lengthen the battery life of the device. He designed a system that could make chips more efficient and patented it.*

Unusual problems had a way of showing up at Ramgopal's doorstep. One day, while interviewing students for admission into IIT-B, one of the faculty members complained of chest pain. Some colleagues took him to the hospital. The doctor suspected that the professor had had a heart attack, but they had to wait for the lab results to prove it.

'As engineers, can't you make a gadget that can detect the cause of chest pain?' the doctor asked the group.

*Today, his patents are being used by semiconductor companies like Infineon Technologies and Intel in Germany to solve problems that engineers face in designing batteries. See Page 33 for more information on patents.

SCIENCE SPEAK

LIFE IN A NANOTECH LAB

IIT-B has a special laboratory called the Centre of Excellence in Nanoelectronics (CEN), where nanodevices are made. It was established in 2006. This is where Ramgopal and his team invented the electronic nose.

Working in a nanoelectronics lab is not easy. Since even a single dust particle can destroy a device, the laboratory follows strict protocols and rules. Every hour, all of the air in the lab is pumped out, filtered and put back in. 'It's the purest air on Earth,' says Ramgopal.

There is a rigorous protocol in place for scientists to go in and out of the lab. Before they enter, scientists need to cover themselves completely

from head to toe. The lab gear includes a chemically resistant lab coat, lab pants, gloves, facemask, safety goggles, head gear and special shoes. It takes up to 20 minutes to dress up. Once inside, scientists cannot eat or use the toilet. To take a lunch or bathroom break, they have to take off all the gear. Before entering the laboratory again, they have to put the protective gear back on.

Since it is such a huge task to get in and out of the laboratory, Ramgopal has fashioned a routine. Every morning, he wears his lab clothes, works for three hours in the lab, and then takes a 20-minute food and toilet break. He heads back into the laboratory again, working for another three-hour stretch.

'We should be able to make a heart attack detector,' one of them said. In the coming weeks, the professors had multiple meetings to discuss how they could create this machine. Ramgopal, who headed the group, visited other departments in the institute and enlisted several professors and students interested in working on the heart attack detector. One of them

was Soumyo Mukherjee from the department of biomedical engineering.

With the help of scientists in the departments of chemistry, computer science and chemical engineering, Ramgopal and Soumyo were able to create a sensor* that could be used to detect cardiac problems. This device would also help Ramgopal develop a bomb sniffer in the near future.

In 2008, when Dr Chidambaram approached Ramgopal, the professor was an established nanodevice expert. However, replacing a sniffer dog with an electronic nose was a tough proposition. A sniffer dog's ability to smell was a million times better than that of a human. Was it possible to make a device that sensitive? Ramgopal and his team worked on it for months and got nowhere.

'You are talking about one particle of an explosive chemical in a billion particles,' said a scientist.

Ramgopal nodded in agreement. It was like finding one person out of more than a billion Indians, instantly, just through smell!

But Shiloh and her amazing nose gave Ramgopal hope, and he began building an electronic nose platform.

Despite the uncertainty, Ramgopal was sure of one thing: he needed all the help he could get. He got in touch with Soumyo, who had worked with him on the heart attack detector. They collaborated with colleagues from different departments at IIT-B.

*A sensor is a device that detects, records and senses changes in the environment around it. The sensor sends this information to electronic systems like a computer.

Ramgopal and his team began building the electronic nose by modifying the structure of the nano heart attack detector. The device they developed was so microscopic that it was 500 times thinner than human hair! A year later, Ramgopal and his team developed a cantilever, a diving-board-like structure that was anchored at one end of the device. The cantilever acted like a signal. It would bend when it sensed a specific molecule, somewhat like the sniffer dog sitting next to a suitcase after smelling a bomb, looking up at its handler.

It was only in 2011 that the team was able to turn the cantilever into a working sensor. Made of substances like silicon compounds and polymers and coated with a special chemical, the sensor could detect the presence of explosives at concentrations as low as a few molecules. It was almost as good as Shiloh's nose!

Ramgopal and his team called it an electronic nose or e-nose. The same year, they founded a start-up, NanoSniff Technologies, which would further develop the sensor and manufacture low-cost detection systems for those who needed a bomb detector, like the army, security forces, and even offices and hotels.

To showcase the gadget at a conference, Ramgopal came up with an innovative idea. He asked his team to create a toy dog which could be attached to the sensor. Now, every time it detected bomb particles, it would bark!

'We have developed an electronic nose that can sniff out bombs,' he told scientists and journalists at the conference. However, a journalist who published the news called it an e-dog instead of an e-nose. Ever since,

the professor's lab has been getting phone calls from children, asking if they can pet his e-dog!

Ramgopal received the Infosys Prize for his invention in addition to more than 25 other prestigious awards from around the world.

After developing the e-nose, Ramgopal is exploring what the other applications of the sensor can be. Can the e-nose be trained like a dog's nose? 'If one of my students has not taken a bath, can I use the e-nose to figure out who it is?' he asked once, laughing. Or can the sensor sniff out if food is fresh or has gone bad? There are hundreds of possible applications, and smelling out explosive chemicals is just one of them.

Ramgopal is currently the director of the Indian Institute of Technology in Delhi (IIT-D). Apart from running the institute, he is also trying to help farmers by creating nanodevices that can tell them how much moisture and nutrients their crops need. His inventions have resulted in the creation of two start-ups that are working in areas like healthcare, security and agriculture. The inventor has plenty of nano plans up his sleeve. But above all, he believes in the power of teamwork. 'Nothing can be done alone. It takes all kinds of scientists to solve a problem,' says Ramgopal to his students.

HOW TO PATENT YOUR INVENTION

A patent is a paper sanctioned by the government that states that a particular scientist has invented a particular machine, or discovered a particular use of a plant and so on.

A patent gives an inventor the right to stop other people from making use of their invention without permission. This is important as an inventor spends years and a lot of money on research to make something new. If scientists patent their work, they can stop other people from copying their inventions and putting them out in the market.

With a patent, a company which is interested in making the product will approach the scientist and offer them money to license the patent. So every time an organization makes money from the scientist's invention, the scientist makes some money too, and can continue their important research work.

To get a patent, a scientist must write down why the invention is unique. This is called a patent application.

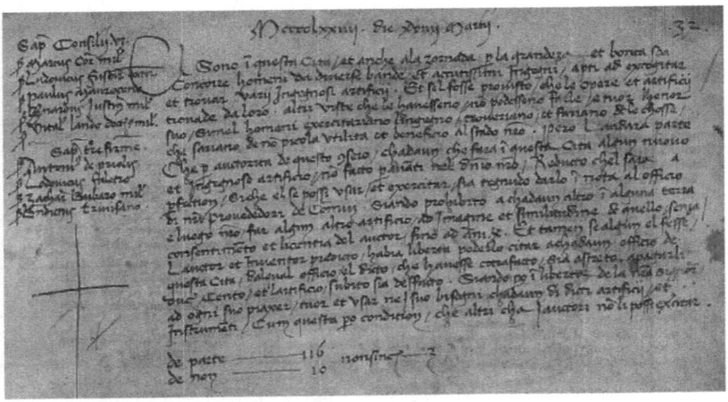

The Venetian Patent Statute, issued by the Senate of Venice in 1474, is one of the earliest patent systems in the world. (Source: Wikimedia Commons)

Once the application is ready, it is sent to the Controller General of Patents, Designs and Trademarks – the Indian government's official body which approves patents. Before the authority awards the patent to an inventor, it will go through other patents to check if the idea is truly original.

Each country issues its own patents. China gives Chinese patents, India gives Indian patents and the USA gives American patents. But an inventor can get a patent in any country of their choice. After decades of inventing nanoelectronics, Ramgopal has 43 patents both in the USA and India!

If you wanted to invent something and patent it, what would it be? Think of 10 things you can invent. Now, research online to find if an inventor has already patented them.

3

A Rainforest in the Middle of a Tea Estate

Wildlife ecologist Divya Mudappa hiked up to the Stanmore rainforest patch in Valparai, Tamil Nadu, and stopped to listen. On a branch close by perched a white-cheeked barbet, incessantly calling out while eating mouthfuls of *Heynea trijuga* – a type of bright red fruit. The trees were just beginning to flower and bear fruit. A pair of Indian scimitar babblers made a ruckus in a bush nearby. A shy pair of Malabar grey hornbills cackled from a dense clump of leaves, eyeing her. Deep in the forest, a Nilgiri langur barked mysteriously.

It was like the whole rainforest had come to welcome her. But upon close inspection, Divya noticed that some quintessential foresty things were missing. There were no great hornbills in the canopy – a large, impressive, colourful, fruit-eating bird that is a threatened species and whose presence would prove the health of a rainforest. The forest floor that the ecologist crouched on was not spongy because there was no leaf litter. The

glistening backs of marching beetles were also missing. The young rainforest that she had created along with her partner and fellow wildlife ecologist, TR Shankar Raman, had still not been accepted fully by the animals and birds.

'It's still young. Give it time,' said Shankar.

'It's been 10 years!' Divya replied, a bit disappointed. She knew she was being impatient.

In 2002, they had planted a sea of saplings on this patch of land, set in the middle of a picturesque tea estate called Stanmore in the Valparai Plateau. Divya's restoration project involved transforming this patch into a dense rainforest. Ten years later, the saplings had grown into trees, but it was still a baby forest. Rainforests are complex ecosystems that grow over hundreds of years, developing an intricate web of relationships between plants, trees, fungi, animals, insects and birds. Could humans ever successfully regrow and restore a rainforest? Divya wondered.

As a child, Divya never imagined that she would spend her life growing rainforests. She grew up surrounded by cats, dogs, bees, snakes and birds. She lived with her parents in a quaint house on the outskirts of Madikeri, a small town in the hills of the Western Ghats in a district called Kodagu (a.k.a. Coorg) in Karnataka. Every evening, after she came back from school, this was her schedule:

- Feed Catty Senior.
- Give a stray dog a belly rub.

- Stop Catty Junior from pouncing on the sparrow that had swooped down to the water trough for a drink.
- Make Catty Junior understand that she's a bad cat.
- Climb the guava tree in the courtyard.
- Watch the coucal hop in the tree. Her dad told her the Kodava name for it was *chambooka*.
- Do homework. *Sigh*.
- Watch a wildlife documentary with her mother. Her favourites were the ones with Jane Goodall.
- Allow Catty Junior to snuggle with her.
- Finish homework; rub another puppy's belly.
- Sit on the porch, listen to the chatter of red-whiskered bulbuls as they went to roost.
- Lazily eye the black spider that was busy making its web.
- Feed Catty Junior.
- Eat dinner.

You can see that her evenings were quite busy. So were her weekends, when Divya and her parents would visit the 15-acre coffee plantation that they owned in Suntikoppa, Kodagu. At the estate, she would wander along the myriad narrow paths, heading deep into the plantations of coffee, oranges and cardamom. The paths were always cool. In Coorg, coffee grows in the shade of big trees like Indian rosewood, fig and pink cedar. All day, Divya would saunter through the estate, exploring every nook and cranny, listening to the birds, playing with insects and collecting leaves.

One summer, when her older brother, who studied in Chennai, was home for the holidays, he joined her on her walks along with their mother, who loved to introduce them to nature. He would stop every few metres to look at a plant or a tree above.

'See this,' their mother exclaimed excitedly, showing them a creeper. 'This is wild pepper. Look how beautiful this ficus* is. Forests are so filled with life!'

Inspired, Divya decided to learn more about forests too. Over the next few years, on her walks through the plantation, she would consciously observe, listen, draw, and note details about the plants and animals she encountered. She watched the birds and insects closely. She observed how the canopy of the fig tree changed colour when the sun went down, or how it became a place full of creatures in the night.

Spring would fill the air with the heady, sweet smells of the white flowers of the coffee plant. Her feet would crunch on dry leaves in autumn. During the monsoon, the trail would become muddy, dotted with bright green shoots. All types of insects, beetles and creepy-crawlies would bustle about in search of food or mates. The ickiest were the leeches. You had to wear your rain boots and be ready for them to crawl up your leg to sneakily suck your blood!

*More commonly known as the fig and closely related to the mulberry tree, ficuses are busy trees in the rainforest, known for their juicy fruits which attract everyone from squirrels to hornbills and wasps.

Sleuth Snoop

I spy another ecologist whose students scan forest floors in the Western Ghats.

By the time Divya was 17, her interest in plants and living organisms had grown immensely. She decided to do a graduate course in zoology in Chennai so that she could continue to learn about plants and animals.

One day, her teacher cut open a sleeping frog in anatomy class, and she saw that its heart was still beating. Horrified, Divya ran out of the lab. Though she knew the course involved dissecting animals, she did not like doing it. She hated cutting open frogs, sharks, lizards, snails, mussels and cockroaches.

'I'm in the wrong course. I can't be violent towards living creatures,' she confided to a friend.

'Let me take you for a turtle walk,' said her friend, putting a consoling arm around her.

In the 1980s, Chennai had an active group of ecologists who went on turtle walks on its beaches.

On the walk, volunteers would introduce visitors to Olive Ridley sea turtles (a type of small sea turtle with an olive-coloured shell) as they arrived from the deep seas to nest along India's eastern coast. After her first walk, Divya decided to join the volunteers who nurtured the turtle eggs and made sure that the hatchlings were released back into the sea and not eaten by dogs. Many a time, little hatchlings would also lose their way and not find the sea because of the bright lights along the shore.

The next year, her schedule got tighter. Every morning, she would attend college, and in the evenings, she would sneak out of the girls' hostel (which had a curfew) to go to the beach and help with turtle conservation.

Divya joined the nature club at her college and went for a camping trip to Guindy National Park in Chennai. There she met Shankar, a student from another college, who could recognize a whole lot of birds from their calls. One night, as they sat around a bonfire, they heard an unusual sound. *Chuk-chuk-chukrrr*.

'Do you know this bird?' asked Divya.

'Oh, you don't?' sniggered Shankar. 'It's a nightjar.'

An angry Divya stomped off. But her curiosity got the better of her and she was back, sitting by Shankar, to understand how he had learnt to recognize so many birds by their sounds. Over the next few months, Divya and Shankar became friends. They met in coffee shops, where he would lend her books about nature and wildlife. Divya would tell him how the fresh batches of turtle hatchlings that had emerged from their eggs undertook

their long march of 20 metres towards the sea from the turtle hatchery in Neelankarai in Chennai.

In 1992, Divya joined Pondicherry University for a postgraduate course in ecology and environmental sciences. Within a year, she knew it was the right field for her. She helped rescue animals, learnt about butterflies and maintained aquariums in the schools nearby.

Sometime during her second year, Divya took up a project to study Malabar grey hornbills in Topslip, a hillstation located in the Anamalai Tiger Reserve (ATR) in the Western Ghats. She had to go deep into the forest to observe the graceful bird's nest – a dangerous task. The forests of Topslip are home to tigers, sloth bears, gaurs and even elephants. To go into these forests, you have to know where to go and what to do if you encounter one of these wild animals.

To familiarize herself, Divya requested Ganesan, a forest guide from the local tribal community known as the Kadars to assist her in the field. He had grown up in the forests of Topslip and knew all about how the animals behaved there. He knew what berries and tubers you could eat and which ones were poisonous. He knew exactly what to do if you ran into elephants and other animals. He could smell animal scat and figure out how long ago the animal had passed that forest path. He became Divya's tracker and field assistant. Divya wanted to learn everything Ganesan knew. The problem was – he did not like to talk.

'What happens if an elephant comes? Where would we run?' she asked one day as she walked behind him.

WHAT MAKES RAINFORESTS SO SPECIAL?

Among all the forests on Earth, rainforests are the most diverse when it comes to the number of species of animals, birds and plants that inhabit them. A single hectare of rainforest may be home to 100–300 species of trees! Small plants like mosses, ferns and orchids grow on tree barks and leaf surfaces. In the animal world, there are minute mites and springtails in the soil, elephants walking on the ground and hornbills swooping in the forest canopy. All of these species are closely dependent on each other for survival, making the rainforest a dynamic ecosystem.

This forest type is found only in those areas around the equator that have over 2,000 millimetres of annual rainfall over most of the year. Research online and name five of India's tropical rainforests.

____

____

'Sshh! Learn by watching and listening to the forest,' he said sternly.

Sometimes, they would encounter wild animals. Once, when they came across a bear, Ganesan whistled and it retreated into the forest. Another day, they saw a tiger. This time, Divya knew what to do – keep still and allow the animal to pass. Be quiet and listen, she remembered.

For months, Divya and Ganesan travelled deep into the forest. Every day, Divya would sit near a hornbill nest with her binoculars and notebook, and observe the goings-on. She noticed how the female hornbill built a

wall to block herself safely inside the nest, and how the male hornbill would bring fruits from around the forest to feed the female and the chicks.

The more she observed, the more she realized how interconnected the relationships in rainforests were. Hornbills needed trees for the fruits. Trees needed the hornbills to spread their seeds widely through the forest so that new trees could grow.

In 1996, Divya started her doctoral studies at the Wildlife Institute of India (WII) in Dehradun. By this time, she had learned the power of stillness and observation when it came to studying wildlife. Her project involved studying the effects of forest fragmentation* on mammals like brown palm civets, which inhabit the Western Ghats.

'By simply eating seeds and dispersing them, the hornbills and civets are responsible for forest regeneration,' she told Shankar excitedly over the phone.

Divya began work on a project that involved comparing two types of forests. One was the Kalakad-Mundanthurai Tiger Reserve (KMTR), spanning an area of 895 square kilometres, with a large, contiguous rainforest† spread over 400 square kilometres. The second forest, which was fragmented, was on the

*Forests are large, continuous areas covered with trees. Humans divide these forests because we need roads, farms and houses to live in. These parts of forests, broken into patches, are called fragmented forests.

†A contiguous forest is one which continues as a whole. Humans have not interfered in the forest. It is still intact and its trees have not been cut to make roads or farmlands.

Valparai Plateau, adjoining the ATR. This 220-square kilometre plateau had been converted into plantations of coffee, tea, cardamom and eucalyptus about a century ago. Now, only small patches of forests remained. About 45 of them were on lands owned by private companies.

That same year, Divya and Shankar and a few of their ecologist friends founded the Nature Conservation Foundation (NCF), an organization to research and conserve India's wildlife. Soon, Shankar, who was also doing his Ph.D from the Indian Institute of Science (IISc), joined Divya at KMTR.

As Divya analysed the differences between the two forests through studying hornbills and civets, she realized something terrible. When rainforests were left undisturbed – their ecosystem untouched by humans – the animals, insects and plants would grow as they needed to. When human activity interfered, the story was different. Animals, birds and insects suffered when the forests were cut down to make way for tea gardens, as had been the case in the Anamalai region. Some species adapted and grew faster because there was more food. Others would start to die off or reduce in numbers because there was no food for them. It was hard on all kinds of creatures, from tiny frogs to huge elephants.

However, Divya's study also showed her something marvellous. Animals and plants could thrive if a rainforest patch was restored with native trees, climbers, other plants and streams of water, and the weeds were taken out – no matter how small it was.

Spot and Colour All 15 Animals

RAINFOREST LAYER CAKE

There are many layers to the rainforest, each inhabited by different species of insects, animals and plants. There's the subsoil, below-ground community of microbes, fungi and burrowing animals. The second layer is formed by the leaf litter on the ground. The third is the above-ground layer, which consists of vegetation like shrubs, ferns, fungi and ground orchids. As you go higher, there's the understory of trees, the mid-story, and finally the topmost layer, called the canopy, which receives most of the natural sunlight. Then, there are the really tall trees, which poke out of the canopy – these towering giants are called emergent trees.

There is a solid network of relationships between animals, birds and trees. For example, the trees give shelter to a lot of animals and birds, including hornbills, bats, monkeys and squirrels. But it isn't a one-sided relationship. The hornbills and monkeys eat fruit and take the tree's seeds into their gullets or cheek pouches, as they move away from the mother tree. The seeds are then dropped at different locations in

the forest where they can grow into saplings and future trees!

The fungi and mushrooms in the soil decompose the fallen litter, along with the beetles. Ecologists have discovered that fungi are the biodiversity police of the rainforest. They make sure that no one tree or plant species becomes dominant. If there's a part of the rainforest where there is a monopoly of the same type of trees, fungi begin to grow faster there, stopping any additional growth.

Scientists know very little about the rainforests and the interdependence of various species. For example, we don't know yet what relationship elephants have with moss, or how fungi communicate with every part of the rainforest.

Even as we rush to discover more, the rainforests around us are being destroyed. Over 100 million hectares across the world have already been lost or severely degraded because of human destruction. Humans are cutting down trees, starting crop fires, mining the Earth's crust, making roads and reservoirs by cutting through forests and so on.

Thankfully, conservation projects are now trying to save these fragile ecosystems from further destruction.

One day, Divya and Shankar were birdwatching in Valparai. 'Let's grow a rainforest here,' she said. Being an ecologist, Shankar understood her desire, but also knew that ecological restoration projects were especially hard because rainforests were such complex ecosystems.

'Are you sure? It will take decades to restore a rainforest,' he said. If Divya was serious, it meant they would have to live in Valparai for a long time, regrowing the forest. She thought for a bit, her mind replaying the significant moments of her life. She realized how rainforests had felt like home to her and brought her true happiness. Divya nodded; she really wanted to do this. It could take her a lifetime, but if she could develop the rainforests so that the native wildlife species returned to it, it would be well worth the effort.

In 2000, Divya and Shankar decided to work on forest restoration in the Valparai plateau and started an NCF rainforest research station in the hill town. They hoped that this research base would attract ecologists and researchers to help out with their rainforest research and restoration efforts.

The first step was to note down what plants and animals lived in a rainforest relatively untouched by human activity. Adjoining the Valparai Plateau is the Anamalai Tiger Reserve, which has been protected by the Forest Department since the early 1970s. The untouched forests within Anamalai Tiger Reserve became their reference site.

The second step was to convince one of the tea companies that owned the land to give them a patch

that was not being used to cultivate tea. In 2001, Hindustan Lever set aside a forest patch for biodiversity conservation. Divya and Shankar were permitted to restore the degraded patch with native rainforest trees. It was a whopping 25 hectares – that's 720 buses parked side-by-side! They called it the Stanmore patch.

The forest had very few trees and was infested with weeds and grass. Surrounded by eucalyptus trees and large expanses of tea plantations, it was a destroyed piece of land, which had forgotten that it had been a rainforest in the past. The two scientists could not wait to get started on it.

'Let's focus on the native trees first,' said Divya.

'Yes,' agreed Shankar, 'the trees are the most important part of a rainforest.'

Trees were, indeed, the life of a rainforest. A single hectare of a rainforest contained at least 80 varieties of trees. Divya was convinced that if she could plant trees in the diverse mix that naturally occurred in the region's forests, small mammals, birds and insects would return to them. Every day, they went to a patch in the Anamalai forests, taking an inventory of the species of trees, plants and animals that they found. Finally, they had a definitive list of the native trees they needed to plant in Stanmore.

To plant trees, they needed saplings, for which they needed seeds. Divya, Shankar and their team combed the Valparai area on foot. They walked along the trails at the edge of the forest, collecting seeds that had dropped from the trees. They drove on roads, scouring the edges

for seeds. They discarded bad seeds – those attacked by fungus and pests or which were simply rotten – and only kept the fresh ones. Their favourite seeds were found under bat roosts and those pooped out by civets. For some reason, these seeds were especially easy to germinate and turn into saplings!

Altogether, they collected 180–190 seed varieties, a combination of shrubs and small to medium-sized trees that could form the understory of the rainforest. Then, there were some from larger trees to form the topmost canopy of their forest. There were also seeds from woody climbers or lianas that typically grow in rainforests.

As soon as they collected the seeds, they had to pot them as forest seeds decay really quickly. They started a nursery near the Stanmore patch – a slow, painstaking process. The nursery had to be protected from rodents and snails which would attack and eat the seeds before they could become saplings. Some seeds took nearly a year to germinate! As they were writing their all-important theses for their Ph.Ds, Divya and Shankar were also busy making sure rodents were not eating the seeds they had just potted!

In 2002, the first round of saplings was ready. But before they could plant them in the Stanmore patch, they had more work to do. The land was covered with invasive weeds like lantana, grasses and vines, which had to be removed. They hired helpers, called their assistants and friends, and headed to the area armed with sickles and machetes. The motley crew cleared the land by removing the weeds and uprooting the lantana

so that it could not regrow there. Finally, the first set of saplings were planted in clusters made up of different species in an imitation of the natural composition of a rainforest.

Over the next few years, they monitored these trees to make sure they were growing well. Would the seedlings survive? Would the rainforest recover? Did small animals like rodents come to nose through its soil? Did snails and bats return? What about the bees and beetles? The biggest sign that the rainforest was well and truly accepted would be when great hornbills arrived in the forest, flapping their large wings, bringing seeds from distant rainforests into the new patch. Or when the tiny beetles marched in, planting eggs on the spongy forest floor.

While they took care of Stanmore, Divya and Shankar also began to plant trees in new patches of land in other tea gardens in Valparai. By 2004–05 two more companies had given them patches of land to turn into rainforests.

'We have 35 more patches of land to plant trees on!' exclaimed Divya. They also moved to a bigger plant nursery, where they grew 160 species of trees and lianas to restore rainforests.

In November 2017, Divya and Shankar revisited the Stanmore patch, the first rainforest they had created. Divya hiked up and stopped to listen, exactly how Ganesan had taught her. The white-cheeked barbet and Indian scimitar babblers were there. So were the Malabar grey hornbills and Nilgiri langurs.

Batty cat cracks

DEFINITE DON'TS FOR WILDIES

- Don't say hello: Wildies are not neighbourhood dogs looking for a pat. We prefer social distance. Capisce?
- Please don't try to rub a wildie's belly. Ugh. Remember, social distance.
- Don't shriek or panic. It does not smell nice.
- Don't feed wildies. Your food stinks.
- A selfie is a no-no. No one likes flashes.

Suddenly, they heard a heavy flapping of wings, high up in the sky. Divya and Shankar craned their necks. With a thump, a large great hornbill flew into the young forest, sitting on the canopy of a fig tree.

'It's a great hornbill!' whispered Divya. 'We've done it!'

'Yes,' answered Shankar. 'We've created a rainforest.'

The great hornbill brought seeds from faraway forests and dropped them into the Stanmore patch. Its presence was proof that the forest which the ecologists had built had been accepted by the mammals and birds of Anamalai hills. 'Let's make more of these,' gushed Divya.

COMBATING CLIMATE CHANGE NATURALLY

For the last 150 years, human industrial activity has begun to produce greenhouses gases. Forests have been chopped to make cities and farms. Coal, oil and natural gases have been burned to produce energy to run our cars and airplanes.

All this frenetic urbanization has increased the level of carbon dioxide in the atmosphere by more than 31 per cent. This makes the atmosphere warmer, leading to global warming and environmental disasters like wildfires, droughts and heatwaves.

Scientists have recently begun to explore how this extra carbon dioxide can be extracted from the atmosphere and trapped so as to reverse global warming. This process is called carbon sequestration or carbon dioxide removal.

One of the most effective methods for carbon sequestration is afforestation and reforestation. Forests are natural carbon dioxide trappers. The trees, plants and shrubs grab hold of the carbon dioxide in the atmosphere and pack it into their roots and the soil around them.

Ecological restoration, the kind that Divya is doing in Valparai, which uses native species, is effective for carbon storage as well as biodiversity conservation. The 70 hectares of restored forests in Valparai, over the last 20 years, have managed to trap 5,000 tons of carbon in them! That's equal to the carbon released by 7.8 million litres of petrol. Recreating forests is the best way to combat climate emergency!

HORRIBLE HAIKU

Rich forest floor
A little beetle farts
Croaking the frog

Recreating rainforests was addictive, and she didn't want to stop.

Divya still loves growing rainforests. By early 2020, Divya and her team had planted 80,000 trees on 300-plus hectares of land – a forest in itself. Their nursery also provides saplings of native trees to the coffee and tea estates of Valparai. Now Divya's organization, NCF, has started recreating rainforests in and around Pakke Tiger Reserve in Arunachal Pradesh. In six years, they have planted 25,000 seedlings and saplings of native trees in the region.

Though the ecologists are doing their best to recreate rainforests, they know they have a long way to go. There are still some differences that Divya sees in the restored forests she creates and the original ones. After all, rainforests take hundreds of years to grow. Divya continues to do her bit, but hopes that other humans start valuing rainforests and protecting them too.

Draw Yourself as an Ecologist

Before she ventures into the rainforest, Divya wears dull-coloured clothing – a colour scheme made up of browns, greys and greens. She puts on boots and leech socks over her trousers. Her gadget must-haves are a pair of binoculars, a GPS system, a notebook, a pen and a camera. She also has an umbrella or a rainproof coverall for those unexpected rains. She always carries a snack, a headlamp, a stick to poke things and a bottle of water with her.

What kind of gear would you pack if you are exploring a forest? Do a little research and draw yourself as an eco-warrior.

4

A Rocket to Poke Martians

The year was 1975. It was a cool, summer evening in Lucknow. A sweaty eight-year-old Anil Bhardwaj trailed behind his older brother and his friends, dragging his cricket bat behind him. They had just won a cricket game against the other kids in the neighbourhood and were returning home, happy and spent.

The sun had set, and a full, bright moon hung low in the sky. Anil stopped to stare at the silvery globe. He noticed that a web of dark shapes swirled on its surface. With a little more staring, the shapes began to look like a round face with a snout, with two long ears popping out of it.

'Look at the moon, Bhaiya!' exclaimed Anil. 'There's a rabbit there!'

'They're just dark spots, Anil,' his brother said, continuing his conversation with his friends.

Anil wasn't convinced. What were those spots on the moon? he wondered. For the next few weeks, he decided

to investigate the mystery of the rabbit on the moon. Every night, he would hurry out to the courtyard of his home to observe and track the moon. He jotted down how it changed its shape, size, colour and position in the sky in a notebook.

Soon, looking up at the night sky became a hobby. Anil began to add in the stars and the constellations that he could spot. His brother joined him in these astronomical adventures. They wrote down the positions of different planets – identifying them as bright objects in the sky that did not twinkle. The stargazers observed the movements of Venus, the positions of constellations as they popped up in different parts of the sky and the phases of the moon as it waxed and waned. Anil pored over the astronomy books in his school library and took the help of his science teacher to understand what he was observing.

Finally, he cracked the mystery! The dark spots on the moon – the ones that looked like a giant rabbit – were places on the lunar surface where ancient volcanoes had erupted billions of years ago.

Although the rabbit mystery was solved, Anil continued to be fascinated by the celestial body* closest to Earth. It astonished him that although astronauts had landed on its surface, there was still so much that was unknown about Earth's moon.

When he became a teenager, Anil was as bewitched by electronics as he was with all things lunar. Much to

*A celestial body is any natural body outside Earth's atmosphere. Examples are moon, sun and other planets in our solar system.

the dismay of his parents, he would wander around the house taking apart household appliances so he could look at their insides.

One day, his mother found that their steam iron had been tampered with. 'Anil! What did you do?' she cried out, knowing well that he was the culprit.

'I wanted to know how it heats, steams and irons!' he said, hiding the transistor component he was cradling in his hands.

By the time Anil enrolled in college, his interest in electronics had grown into a full-blown passion. At Lucknow University, while he was studying physics, maths and statistics, he even developed a small transistor, putting it together from scratch by soldering its components.

A big turning point came when Anil turned 18. A scientist from the USA came home for dinner with his parents. The visitor entertained the family with colourful stories of his adventures in science. That night, an inspired Anil resolved to become a scientist. 'I want to research celestial bodies,' he announced to his parents. And he went on to do just that.

The year 1986 was an extraordinary one for space lovers. Amateur astronomers across the world were getting ready for a rare celestial event: the Halley's Comet was slated to make an appearance in the Earth's neighbourhood. It was a once-in-a-lifetime event as the comet, which revolved around the sun, was visible from Earth only once every 75–76 years.

THE HARE AND THE MOON

Most ancient folklore has stories about a rabbit on the moon. In Far Eastern folklore, Jade Hare is a mythical figure who lives on the moon. He holds a mortar and pestle and pounds herbs for the immortals who live there.

Like Anil, countless people through the ages had observed the dark spots on the moon. Ancient astronomers thought that they were seas or lakes on its surface. Scientists now know that the spots are basaltic plains formed by ancient volcanic eruptions. They reflect less light than the highlands surrounding them, and look like dark spots if you look at the moon from the Earth without a telescope.

The next time the moon is full, look at it and observe the dark shapes on its lower side. Can you see the hare busy making herbal medicines for the immortal lunar folk?

Anil and his friends went to a small observatory in Lucknow to witness the astronomical spectacle. The group held a night-long stakeout and were rewarded with the sight of the fiery comet, its long tail blazing across the sky.

'What is it made of?' Anil wondered. Within a few years, scientists had found the answer to his question. The glorious sight of the comet streaking across space was etched in his memory, and would go on to become a big part of his research in astrophysics.

Inspired by his encounter with the Halley's Comet, Anil decided to study a curious phenomenon called 'airglow'* at the Indian Institute of Technology, Banaras Hindu University (BHU), where he was pursuing a doctorate or a Ph.D in physics. His focus was on a little-known aspect called the 'coma', the hazy atmosphere surrounding a comet, which was made up of a cloud of gas, ice and dust. He also researched another fascinating occurrence – the aurora. Auroras are brilliant, multihued lights appearing across the sky in the polar regions of planets with magnetic fields, just like Earth. Auroras could happen on comets as well, and Anil studied them further.

Apart from a visit by the Halley's Comet, the year 1986 saw other exciting developments in space science. For the first time ever, observational data from the faraway planet Uranus was beamed back to Earth by *Voyager 2*. In 1977, the National Aeronautics

*Airglow is a faint emission of light by a planetary atmosphere.

and Space Administration (NASA) launched *Voyager 2*, a fly-by* space probe to study the outer planets – Jupiter, Saturn, Uranus and Neptune. It had taken 12 years for *Voyager 2* to reach Neptune! This was due to a rare alignment of the outer planets. Otherwise it would have taken *Voyager 2* almost three times the 12 years it took to reach Neptune.

As data from Uranus reached NASA by 1986, Anil was one of the few Indian scientists to study it. It took him a year to analyse this data, as in the 1980s, the technology to analyse massive datasets was limited. He didn't have a personal computer or a laptop. So he would head to the computer centre at his institute every morning, where he would give the operator punched cards with typed codes written on them. The operator would run the codes on the computer, and Anil would return to the lab in the evening to look at them.

Phew! It was hard work, but well worth the trouble to discover the secrets of Uranus. Along with other scientists, Anil's research uncovered the presence of a layer of bright light in Uranus's atmosphere, a phenomenon which was named 'electroglow'.

Having completed his doctoral research on auroras, outer planets, comets and faraway celestial bodies, Anil landed his first job as a scientist at the Space Physics Laboratory at the Vikram Sarabhai Space Centre (VSSC), in Thiruvananthapuram, Kerala.

*A fly-by probe is a robotic spacecraft that does not go into orbit around a planet but flies past it.

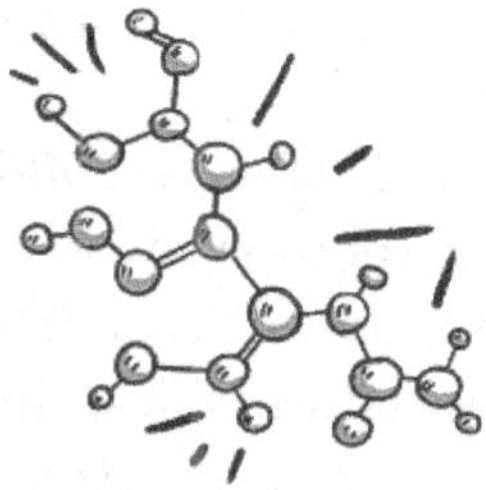

SCIENCE SPEAK
CHASING COMETS

The Halley's Comet has been observed by skygazers since 240 BCE. Ancient astronomers from China, Babylon, India and Greece saw the same object appear in the sky. The comet was eventually named in English after astronomer Edmond Halley, who was the first to discover that it appeared near the Earth every 75–76 years.

While Anil and his fellow space enthusiasts were gazing at the Halley's Comet, something equally remarkable was happening elsewhere. Five space missions from Europe, the Soviet Union and Japan (nicknamed the 'Halley Armada') journeyed close to the comet to collect data – something that hadn't been attempted before. Space scientists analysed it to find that that the comet was made up of a mixture of volatile ices – water, carbon dioxide, ammonia – and lots of dust. When this cocktail of ice sublimates (converts directly from solid to gaseous state) as Halley's Comet approaches the sun, it leaves a long trail of light in the sky. That's the comet's tail!

The state-of-the-art laboratory explored how physics worked in different planetary atmospheres. He continued studying comets and outer planets at VSSC, and soon became a leading expert on space and planetary sciences in India.

Cut to the early 2000s. The Indian Space Research Organisation (ISRO), the country's premier space agency, was planning to expand India's planetary exploration program. In 2003, a group of leading space scientists from around the country met in Bengaluru and decided to launch India's first moon mission. Anil was one of the scientists present at this historic meeting. This was the opportunity that he had been waiting for! He could finally build his own experiment – called a 'payload' – and send it to the moon to collect the kind of data he had dreamed of as a child.

By 2003, ISRO had begun readying India's first mission to the moon – Chandrayaan–1 (or 'moon vehicle' in Sanskrit). Anil jumped at the chance to probe the moon's surface up-close. He put in a proposal for a payload with the Chandrayaan–1 team. It was not only approved, but Anil was also made the principal investigator or the lead scientist to create a payload called a Sub-keV Atom Reflecting Analyzer – SARA for short. SARA was a collaboration between the Space Physics Laboratory at VSSC where Anil worked and scientists from Sweden, Japan and Switzerland.

First on the agenda, the scientists had to figure out which part of the lunar science they wanted to analyse.

They unanimously agreed to study how the solar wind interacts with the moon's surface.

The payload was built over the course of four years by various teams around the world. As this was a pioneering experiment, the team had to devise special techniques and specific instruments.

Developing an experiment that could work in outer space was a tricky matter. The biggest challenge was designing a payload that could withstand the harsh conditions of space. What materials would they use? How would they shape the payload to fit it onto Chandrayaan–1? How much would it weigh? What kind of components, sub-systems and sensors would they include?

SARA was developed in three parts – two were made in Sweden and one in Anil's laboratory. It was neither

Batty Cat Cracks

Dr Space Man, are there rats on the moon? Batty can weather the cold and no oxygen, but a world without mice is forlorn.

heavy nor big. Weight in space is expensive, and so the scientists were careful to keep the payload light. It weighed 4.5 kilograms and could fit into a small box.

The payload was tested in a special vacuum chamber in Anil's lab. The chamber simulated the conditions that the probe would encounter in outer space, from the pressure to the harsh temperature environment. SARA was tested for several days and nights. The tests were successful, and SARA was finally ready to take off!

Anil and his team travelled to the ISRO campus in Bengaluru to fit the payload onto Chandrayaan–1. SARA went up on the top deck. The sensors were so placed that once Chandrayaan–1 reached the moon, SARA could see in two directions - one towards the moon's surface and one facing the solar wind (sun).

D-day dawned on 22 October 2008 at the Satish Dhawan Space Centre at Sriharikota, an island off the coast of Bay of Bengal in Andhra Pradesh. Chandrayaan–1, India's first lunar probe, was ready to take off. The met department had predicted heavy rain showers, adding to the worries of the already nervous scientists. Despite the bleak weather, Anil could feel the electricity in the air. The 500-odd scientists, engineers, technicians and analysts who had gathered for the launch of India's first moon mission knew they were creating history!

ISRO scientists decided to press ahead with the launch, rain or no rain. At 6.22 a.m., a rocket called the PSLV-XL, with Chandrayaan–1 aboard, took off into the skies. The ground shook as it shot up, escaping the heavy grey clouds. Anil grabbed hold of a pole to steady himself.

RENDEZVOUS WITH A ROCKET

The 1960s were a turbulent decade for India. The young democracy faced a host of challenges, like food shortages, political hardship and a war with China. Against this backdrop, two of the country's most well-known scientists from the department of atomic energy, Homi Bhabha and Vikram Sarabhai, approached the then prime minister, Jawaharlal Nehru, with the idea to launch a space initiative.

The project was approved and Vikram connected with fellow scientists from around the world to launch India's first space rocket. It was made in bits and pieces – the basic rocket and tracking equipment came from the USA, a computer and a helicopter were sourced from the Soviet Union, and a payload was created by space scientists in France.

Next, Vikram scouted for an open stretch of land from where the rocket could take off. He zeroed in on Thumba, a quiet fishing village near Thiruvananthapuram. The only usable building in the hamlet, the Mary Magdalene Church, was converted into a workshop. Scientists from around India were hired to work on the site. Together, they developed the first launching station in the country – the Thumba Equatorial Rocket Launching Station (TERLS). On 21 November 1963, a small rocket, the Nike-Apache, took off from Thumba, creating space history for India.

In 1969, Vikram's space initiative was renamed the Indian Space Research Organisation (ISRO). Since then, ISRO has launched many more rockets and spacecraft. In 1975, it built India's first space satellite, Aryabhata. In 2008, ISRO sent an unmanned lunar orbiter, Chandrayaan-1, into orbit around the moon. In 2013, it launched Mangalyaan, the Mars Orbiter Mission, which entered the orbit of the red planet (as Mars is also known). It launched India's second moon mission, Chandrayaan-2, in 2019. ISRO has a busy diary for the future of space exploration, including a mission to the sun, Venus and sending astronauts into space.

Everyone cheered. Ten minutes later, just as the spacecraft reached the end of Earth's atmosphere, it started to rain. Chandrayaan–1 did not feel the rain. It was already on its way to the moon!

It took 14 days for Chandrayaan–1, carrying 11 payloads from countries like the USA, Germany and Bulgaria to reach the moon's orbit. By January 2009, data from SARA started to come in – Anil couldn't wait to study it and crack the moon's mysteries.

The data offered new insights on how the solar wind interacted with the lunar surface. As the SARA team went through it, they discovered something unusual. As the moon doesn't really have an atmosphere of its own, the solar wind or high-energy particles from the sun that hit the lunar surface behave differently. Anil concluded that charged particles from the sun hit the surface at 400 km/second, are converted into neutral particles, and thrown back into the space around the moon. Researchers could now make intelligent guesses about the types of processes happening on the moon by studying these particles.

Over the next few years, Anil and fellow space researchers began planning other deep space missions. From the many ideas that were bounced around, scientists at ISRO zeroed in on a mission to Mars. Unlike the moon, Mars presented fresh challenges, like its distance from Earth (a close approach distance of more than 62 million kilometres) and its elliptical orbit, which further increased its distance from Earth.

Foxy Facts

EYEING A PLANET. FAR. FAR AWAY...

How do we know things about distant planets or our closest neighbour, the moon? It's all thanks to the spacecraft that we have sent out, like Chandrayaan-1 that orbited Earth's moon, or NASA's fly-bys, *Voyager 1* and *Voyager 2*, that visited the outer planets.

These spacecrafts carry experiments called payloads, which carry scientific instruments and equipment like sensors and cameras that record data and send it back to Earth through radio waves (called downlink). This data is then analysed by space scientists like Anil to deepen our knowledge of the universe.

Sleuth Snoop

I spy another engineer who makes sensors only at a nano level. Which chapter mentions them?

____

But Indian scientists were unfazed and made a bold proposal for a Mars orbiter.

In 2012, Anil got a call that left him astounded. ISRO had gotten the go-ahead from the Government of India for a Mars mission. This was to be India's first interplanetary adventure, and he was asked to be a principal investigator once again! Named Mars Orbiter Mission (MOM), it is better known as Mangalyaan ('Mars-craft' in Sanskrit).

To send a mission to this faraway celestial body, space scientists had to get the timing right. As the orbit of Mars is elliptical, they had to make sure that the spacecraft reached the planet when it was closest to Earth, also known as the close approach distance. After carefully calculating the distance, time of arrival and orbit, they worked out that a brief window of opportunity opened

up once every two years. Without any time to waste, it was decided that the orbiter had to be launched by November 2013.

'But that's just 18 months away!' said a panicky Anil to his colleagues at the Space Physics Laboratory. It felt like an impossibly short time to narrow down on the area of study, design the payload and build it. But Anil couldn't afford to miss out – if India was sending a mission to Mars, he was determined to send a payload with it.

Along with the scientists in his laboratory, he began to develop the Mars Exospheric Neutral Composition Analyzer (MENCA) to study the atmosphere of Mars. The 10-member team plunged headlong into the gargantuan task of building the payload. The team hurried to create a prototype. Once it was ready, the payload was tested in a vacuum chamber.

But something was amiss. The payload wasn't collecting data in the way that it should. Anil puzzled over what may have gone wrong. He rubbed his sleep-deprived eyes. The team had been working non-stop for months now, and everyone was exhausted.

Anil decided to take a break and went home in the middle of the day, much to his wife's surprise. He sat in his garden, deep in thought. He looked and looked at his notes, tired and a little frustrated. What had gone wrong? Why was the data incorrect? Even a tiny miscalculation meant that they would fail and would not be able to participate in the Mars mission.

Sometime in the middle of the night, the answer hit a sleepy Anil. They were testing it differently! He rushed

back to the laboratory. Others on the team joined him in the wee hours of the night. Anil made a change in the technique with which they were testing the payload. Much to everyone's relief, the instrument started to work just fine. They tested MENCA again over the course of several days and nights. Finally, when it was ready, the team flew to the ISRO centre in Bengaluru to fit it onto the Mangalyaan.

On 5 November 2013, Anil was back at the Satish Dhawan Space Centre at Sriharikota for another epic day. Outside the bustling control centre, the MOM stood in its launch vehicle, glistening in the sun and ready to shoot up into the skies. Over 500 scientists and technicians from ISRO were working round the clock to iron out last-minute glitches. The atmosphere in the control room was tense.

Finally, at 2.38 p.m., the PSLV-C25 rocket, with the Mars orbiter aboard, lifted off in a haze of cloud, dust and heat. Anil felt the ground beneath him vibrate, matched by the hammering of his own heart. Forty-five minutes later, Mangalyaan reached the Earth's orbit. Anil and his team were ecstatic; the last few months of gruelling work had paid off.

After a 10-month voyage, the MOM reached its destination. On 24 September 2014, it latched onto the planet's orbit with precision. As data from Mars began to stream in, Anil knew the mission had been a smashing success. India became the only country in the world that had successfully inserted an orbiter around Mars on its first attempt. Over the next

five years, Mangalyaan would send two terabytes of imaging data for scientists like Anil to pore over.

Meanwhile, an excited Anil got busy scrutinizing the information that was being transmitted by the payload. Due to the unique trajectory of the MOM's orbit around Mars, Anil had the rare chance to study the evening side of the planet. Just as he had with Chandrayaan-1, he stumbled on something unusual.

'The data suggests that the carbon dioxide-dominated atmosphere is converted to an oxygen-dominated exosphere near 270 km on the dusk (evening) side of Mars,' Anil concluded in his findings. He had uncovered something new and previously unknown. This changed the dynamics of how the atmosphere of Mars would come to be studied.

India's space adventure continues, and Anil is right at the heart of the action. In 2019, ISRO launched Chandrayaan-2, another mission to the moon, for which he created a payload called Chandra's Atmospheric Composition Explorer (CHACE-2). Currently, he is the director of the Physical Research Laboratory (PRL) set up by Vikram Sarabhai to research cosmic rays in Ahmedabad.

At PRL, Anil is busy developing a slew of new payloads. The most exciting of them is for ISRO's upcoming mission, Aditya-L1, which will study the sun! He is also part of an elite group of Indian space scientists from ISRO who are preparing to send a spacecraft to Venus, another one to Mars and a manned mission to the moon.

For all his incredible achievements in the world of space science, Anil has been awarded the Shanti Swarup Bhatnagar Prize, the Infosys Prize and the Outstanding Achievement Award from ISRO. He still faces challenges every day, but he knows that if he works hard and stays inspired, anything is possible. 'You have to have fire!' is a catchphrase he uses to encourage his colleagues at the lab.

Like the little boy who marvelled at the moon, Anil continues to be enchanted by lunar enigmas. Some day, he hopes to study the deep freeze environment on the moon and discover more about the mysterious dark patches that continue to fascinate him.

Match the Spacecraft

Space is not easy to navigate. It is hostile and dangerous. That's why scientists have to be careful when they're designing spacecraft. Match the spacecraft listed below to their descriptions.

1. ROVER	A. This spacecraft does not orbit around a planet but flies past it. Its instruments collect data as it passes a planet, which is then sent back to Earth.
2. LANDER	B. A spacecraft designed to travel to a distant planet and enter into orbit.
3. FLYBY	C. A short mission spacecraft that collects data about the atmosphere of a planet or its satellite as it passes through it.
4. SPACE OBSERVATORY	D. A spacecraft designed to reach the surface of a planet and survive long enough to send data back to Earth.
5. ATMOSPHERIC PROBE	E. These are designed to land and move around a planet's surface, collecting data.
6. ORBITER	F. This one does not leave the Earth's orbit. It stays in orbit around the Earth, observing distant galaxies and celestial objects.

I Spy with a Telescope

Fill in the crossword with the names of celestial bodies that we can observe around us.

ACROSS

4. Small rocky objects that orbit around the sun (8)
5. A shining spheroid of plasma held by its own gravity (4)
6. A shooting star (6)

DOWN

1. A celestial object with a recognized orbit around a planet (9)
2. A system of stars, dust, dark matter and stellar fragments (6)
3. An icy object that has a long tail when it travels close to the sun (5)

5

A Machine to Annoy Plants

It was the year 1865. Nine-year-old Jagadish Chandra Bose was sent to a boarding school in Kolkata. The boy had no friends there. No one in the school spoke Bengali, the only language he knew. Everyone spoke English, and he didn't know any at the time.

Jagadish missed his family and his house in Bardhaman, a small town in West Bengal, where his parents lived. He also missed his friends from the primary school he had attended. What he missed most, though, were the plants in his garden.

Every day after lessons at his new school, Jagadish would hide in the small garden behind his hostel and talk to the plants that grew there. His favourite was a weed called *Mimosa pudica*. Popularly known as the touch-me-not, the shy plant's leaves turned inwards when they were touched.

Jagadish would spend hours playing with the *Mimosa pudica*'s leaves, observing their movement as he stroked

them. As soon as he flicked them with his fingertips, the leaves would fold into themselves. It really looked like the plant wanted to hide away!

It's exactly like me! he thought.

One afternoon, after science class, he approached his teacher. 'Do plants have feelings?' he asked.

'It's not been proven...yet,' answered the teacher, with a twinkle in his eye.

Now, the 1860s were a long, long time ago. Though scientists had discovered a lot about plants by then, they definitely didn't think plants could feel. *Animals* had feelings, they believed. If you tickled a cat, it purred. If you poked a pig, it oinked in annoyance. If you rubbed a dog's ears, it let out a low, pleasurable whine.

Human beings were the same, scientists thought back then. They cried, felt pain, reacted to the environment and each other. But how did plants react? Plants were there to be eaten, thank you very much, your average scientist in 1865 would say!

But young Jagadish vehemently disagreed. He saw how the weather affected the plants around him. 'They brighten up when the sun shines on them, and droop when the gardener forgets to water them. Of course they have feelings!' he insisted. Their reaction was just different from that of animals and humans.

Jagadish grew up to be a highly inquisitive adult, filled with questions. At that time, India was still under British rule. There weren't too many universities in the country then, so well-to-do families sent their children to Britain for higher education. Once they graduated,

most families wanted their children to pass the Indian Civil Service examination and join the administrative staff of British India.

But Jagadish's father wanted him to become a scholar. Jagadish readily agreed – after all, he wanted to find out more about plants and their feelings. He travelled to the UK to study natural sciences* at the University of Cambridge. At the university, he became really interested in physics. He learnt how to design and build scientific instruments, which could help observe the world around him. Armed with this equipment and knowledge, he planned to study phenomena in physics and plant biology, his two big passions.

In 1885, the physicist-botanist-and-biologist returned to Kolkata and became a physics professor at Presidency College. Putting to use all that he had studied in the UK, he created a small lab in the college for his experiments. Soon, students from around the country flocked to the lab to conduct research in physics as well as plant biology.

The first thing that Jagadish set out to investigate was the idea of 'irritability'† in plants. As you know, at that time, scientists did not believe that plants felt irritable, or had emotions the way animals and humans did. They only knew of two types of plants – sensitive and normal. Sensitive ones, like touch-me-nots, showed

*Natural science deals with the study of the physical world and natural phenomena, and includes physics, chemistry and biology.

†In science, 'irritability' is a response a living organism gives to a stimulus. In animals, this irritability can be measured by observing how their muscles move.

movement when touched. Normal ones, like a rose bush, did nothing. There was no other classification.

Through observations, Jagadish knew that the reaction or irritability in plants was different from an animal's reactions. *A marigold cannot glower at you when you pull it*, he thought. *A bougainvillea bush cannot cry out in pain when you cut its flowers*.

'But it doesn't mean the plant doesn't feel pain!' Jagadish said to himself.

Determined to prove everyone wrong, he began experimenting on a weed in the neighbourhood – *Biophytum sensitivum*, known as *jhalai* in Bengali. As its name suggested, the weed's leaves were sensitive. They would get excited and twitch, like a muscle, when poked. Jagadish observed that a weak stimulus (a physical touch or change that provoked a reaction) gave rise to a single response. But a stronger stimulus gave rise to a series of responses. So, if he poked the plant, it reacted once. If the plant was badly hurt, however, it reacted many times, and in fact, *remembered* it and kept reacting to the stimuli for years!

In the nineteenth century, there were no machines with which you could measure these reactions or observe what was happening inside a plant's cells*. Jagadish wanted to build a machine to do this, so that he could record their reactions and publish the results in a scientific paper.†

*A plant cell is the basic unit of life of organisms in the plant kingdom.

†A scientific paper is a report written in a particular style, to describe original research results. It's by writing reports that scientists across the world

He ended up inventing two devices that could capture minute plant reactions.

The magnification crescograph was able to gauge tiny movements that a plant made in reaction to something. The resonant recorder measured the little electric charges that went through a plant's leaf and stem when something changed around it.

'Stimulation induces an electric charge in the irritable tissue,' Jagadish noted. If you stabbed a plant's leaf, an electric charge went up from that leaf to the main plant, which showed that the whole plant felt the pain.

With these machines, he was able to prove that plants reacted to physical stimuli and could feel pain. But Jagadish was not satisfied – he wanted to understand the nervous system* of plants more deeply and so developed another machine for it – the conductivity balance.

At this time, scientists used a recording instrument called the kymograph to study variations in physiological phenomena like muscle movement and blood pressure. It consisted of a revolving drum wrapped with a sheet of paper and an attached ink pen. The pen would move each time it sensed a variation, drawing a graph of mountains and valleys on the paper.

---

communicate with each other about new discoveries, why their discovery or invention is important, and how it changes global science and technology.

*Although they insisted plants felt no pain or other feelings, biologists at that time believed plants had a nervous system so that the stem, leaves, branches and roots could communicate with each other.

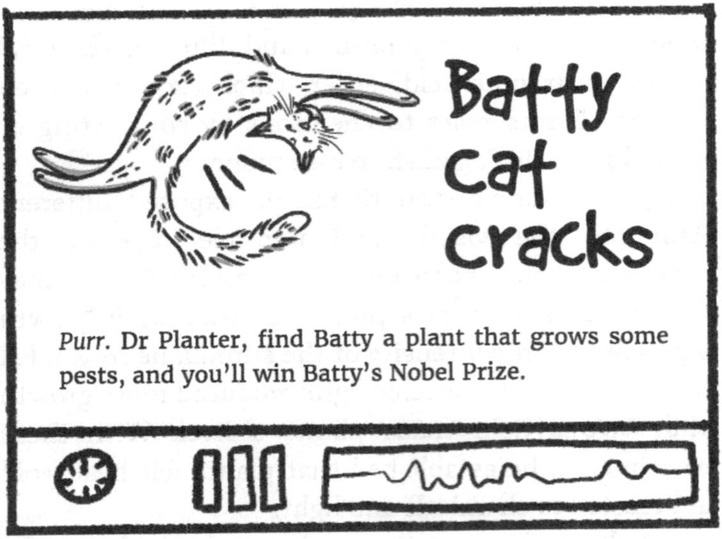

Jagadish reused this machine to develop what came to be known as the conductivity balance, which could record the effects of various kinds of drugs or chemical agents on the nervous system of plants.

Depending on the level of irritability, the ink pen would put a dot on the paper as it moved. After pulling out the long graph, Jagadish would interpret the series of dots. Through this experiment, he found out that when a plant was given a stimulating drug or chemical that increased its physiological activity, its electric charge became quicker. When it was given a depressant or a substance that brought down its activity, the plant's electric charge got slower.

Next, the biologist treated a plant's roots with acid. Using the machine, he measured the electrical response it sent to other parts of the plant. He then exposed

plants to varying temperatures and different chemical agents – carbonic acid, ether, chloroform and even poisons. 'Plants react to chemicals by contracting or expanding,' said Jagadish to his students.

Jagadish didn't stop there. He exposed different plants to the visible and invisible rays of the electromagnetic spectrum* and observed how they responded. Wireless rays† produced variations in growth depending on the intensity of the stimuli, he concluded in his observations. Feeble light produced more growth while strong light made plants shrivel. With these experiments, he established that plants felt heat, cold and reacted to chemicals and light.

Jagadish went on to prove that a plant felt pain by drowning it in a thermal bath or a warm body of water as he slowly increased the temperature. At 60° Celsius, the plant couldn't take the heat anymore; it experienced a violent spasm and died. 'There is an intense electric discharge during death,' he noted down. This electrical release proved that the plant had gone through pain before its death.

One day, while going to college, Jagadish came across a plant that he had first seen as a child. He stopped to watch it in action. Called *Drosera rotundifolia* or sundew, it was a plant that ate insects! The leaves of

*Electromagnetic spectrum is a term used by scientists to describe the entire range of light that exists. From radio waves to gamma rays, most of the light in the universe is invisible to us.

†Wireless rays include radio waves, microwaves from cell phones, laptops, tablets, computers and Wi-Fi.

Sleuth Snoop

I spy a lab in Europe that uses electromagnetic fields to smash things. Name the lab and the scientist who works there.

____

____

the carnivorous plant were covered with tentacles that discharged acid. Any hapless insect which sat on its leaves would get stuck, and the tentacles on the leaf would trap it and suck out its body fluid. Soon, the insect would be dissolved and digested, and only its skeleton would be left behind.

Jagadish was convinced that the leaves of the *Drosera* acted as its stomach. How else could a plant *eat* another living being? The leaves contained acid that dissolved the insect and ingested it.

Do other plants have organs too? he wondered. During his time, scientists knew that the heart was a pumping organ responsible for circulating blood through the body of an animal or human. That's how inhaled oxygen went into the bloodstream and travelled through the body.

HORRIBLE HAIKU

Tickle it does
Till the stem
Whacks the scientist
to a pulp

Scientists also knew that plants had a substance called sap, a transparent gooey fluid inside their stems, which was believed to be the equivalent of blood. Jagadish pondered if he could prove that sap pressure was similar to blood pressure. Did plants have hearts that pumped this sap through their system?

To investigate this, the biologist invented yet another instrument called the optical sphygmograph or plant feeler. It had two rods – one of them was fixed against the stem of the plant, and another moved with the stem of the plant, on the other side. The machine recorded the movement of sap as it was pumped up from the roots towards the leaves and branches. 'The passage of each pulse is attended by an infinitesimal expansion,' Jagadish wrote in his observations.

To put it simply, the stem of the plant bulged every time the sap went up from the roots to the leaves. After each pulse, which expanded the stem, the sap would stop and the stem would return to its normal width. Just like a heartbeat! Jagadish administered a depressant, and the plant's pulse slowed down. When he gave it a stimulant, the sap stream became faster.

This led Jagadish to make an unusual discovery about the nature of plants. He found that plants had a

more complex nervous system than animals and even humans! One drop of hydrochloric acid on the tip of the uppermost leaf of a mimosa plant sent an impulse that travelled all the way through its stem and roots. Through this impulse, its leaves let the main stem know that something was wrong, and the whole plant reacted to it.

By the early 1900s, Jagadish was on a roll. He couldn't stop inventing sophisticated machines to study plants! He made a photosynthetic recorder that was so sensitive that it could detect and record the formation of carbohydrates, or food, on a leaf as soon as it was exposed to sunlight*. The instrument could track this conversion from sunlight to food and measure it.

Then, Jagadish got a little more ambitious. He envisioned a device that could measure the growth of plants. Making it would prove to be a real challenge as plants grew extremely slowly, he discovered.

'Even a snail moves two thousand times faster than a growth in the tip of a leaf,' he exclaimed. 'Plants grow about 1/100000 inch per second!' he wrote in an essay about his research.

To measure the growth of plants, he made the high magnification crescograph, which was able to record growth magnified from ten thousand times to fifty million times. Through the instrument, he found that a plant could grow very slowly one day and

*To carry on living, plants need energy, just like us. However, they do not need to eat food for energy. They have natural solar cells on their leaves, green-coloured cells called chlorophyll, through which they can convert sunlight into food and use it for energy.

Batty cat cracks

Meowr! Jagadish was such a star that scientists named a crater on the moon after him, with a diameter of 91 kilometres! Rather big for an award, no? Imagine lugging it all the way back from the moon on a rocket – that's 3,84,400 kilometres, my juicy rats – and stuffing the behemoth into your showcase of achievements. Phew. Just the thought makes Batty's paws hurt.

very, very slowly the next day. He also found that different plants grew at different rates. If a plant got more sunlight on one day, it would grow faster. If it got less sunlight or if it felt really cold, the plant would grow less on that day.

Jagadish's experiments pushed the frontiers of biophysics*, when this branch of science was practically unheard of. His findings were so groundbreaking that

*Biophysics is an interdisciplinary science that applies approaches and methods traditionally used in physics to study biological phenomena. The term was coined by Karl Pearson in 1892, around the same time that Jagadish was conducting experiments in the field.

A RADIO STAR

Though this chapter talks about Jagadish's research in biology and plants, this part of the scientist's life started later. Before his research into plants, he was already a renowned physicist, known for his pioneering work on radio waves and transistor junctions. Although scientists knew about the physics of light in the nineteenth century, they hadn't discovered the electromagnetic spectrum of invisible rays like radio waves, gamma rays and X-rays.

Jagadish was one of the few scientists in the world who detected radio waves through a self-developed machine: the coherer, a radio signal detector.

The genius physicist was at least 60 years ahead of his time in his inventions. He could have made a lot of money had he patented the coherer. Instead, he published a paper on it and put out the information in the public domain. His work on radio signals would go on to contribute to the development of future technologies, including the radio and wireless communication like your smartphones today!

they forever changed how scientists and biologists perceived plants. 'Plants feel pain and understand love,' he declared. While he could scientifically prove that plants felt pain, the part about love still hasn't been proven. Can *you* prove it?

6

An All-Seeing Electronic Eye

Subhasis Chaudhuri started working in computer vision thanks to his favourite professor. The year was 1984. An engineering student at the Indian Institute of Technology, Kharagpur (IIT-KGP), Subhasis was looking for a project for his final year thesis.

'Sir, can you suggest an interesting problem to work on in the area of computer vision?' he asked Professor Chatterjee.

'I can, but it will be a tough one,' warned the professor.

'That's okay. I'm not scared of tough problems!' replied Subhasis, smiling.

There was a reason why Subhasis was so confident. He had grown up in different villages in Murshidabad in West Bengal, one of the poorest districts in the country. His father, a teacher, would set up schools in different villages, taking his family with him.

Since schools in villages did not offer a high quality of education, Subhasis's father would give his children

tough maths and science problems to solve so they could hone their problem-solving skills. Sometimes, Subhasis would fail to crack them. His father would then help him, encourage him to be patient and tell him to keep trying! In the eleventh standard, Subhasis moved to a boarding school in Kolkata where he continued working with the same spirit. By the time he got into IIT-KGP, he was confident that he could solve difficult problems – a skill that would prove useful to him in the future.

This is why Subhasis was not scared of challenges. Professor Chatterjee gave him a few scientific papers to read on computer vision. He wanted him to find a way through which computers could scan photographs of human eyes and diagnose eye diseases.

Back in 1985, computer vision was a new field. Engineers around the world were excited about the possibilities of exploring how computers *saw* images and videos. Subhasis had first heard about it at a seminar in his college. He was thrilled when Professor Chatterjee gave him a project in this cutting-edge field.

As Professor Chatterjee had warned, the problem was a difficult one. Subhasis needed to develop a computer code* to instruct the computer to see photos of human eyes in a certain way. At this time, IIT-KGP did not have too many computers. Moreover, the processing power of these computers was also slow – way slower than a smartphone's processing capability today. How could

*Writing a code or coding is the process of developing sets of instructions for computers about what actions to perform.

Subhasis work on a project that required a computer to look at hundreds of pictures of a human eye in order to detect a pattern?

The engineering student was not discouraged and dived into his project. But as he reached the end of his course, he hadn't managed to solve the problem. Dejected, he headed to Professor Chatterjee's office.

'I failed,' said Subhasis, slumping into a chair.

'No, you did not. You tried,' the professor answered. 'You can do a lot better next time.'

After completing his graduation, Subhasis did a postgraduate degree in electrical engineering from the University of Calgary, Canada. Next, he joined the University of California, USA, to do a Ph.D. To support himself financially, Subhasis began working at the university's eye hospital. There, he met an eye doctor (called an ophthalmologist) who told him how exhausting it was to look at photos of patients' eyes to check if they had diabetic retinopathy*, a symptom of diabetes.

'It's really tiring,' the doctor said.

'Why can't you automate this?' asked Subhasis. 'A computer should be able to detect diseased blood vessels by viewing photos of the retina.'

'That's what I was hoping you would say,' the doctor said. 'Can you make this happen?'

*In your eye, retina is a membrane that lines the back of the eyeball. It contains millions of light-sensitive cells and nerve cells that receive and organize visual information. Diabetic retinopathy is a disorder caused by diabetes that occurs when high blood-sugar levels damage blood vessels in the retina.

WHAT DO COMPUTERS SEE?

Computer vision is a field of science that deals with how computers can be trained to analyse digital images or videos using artificial intelligence (AI). It is a way to use computers to see the way *humans see.*

Scientists working in the domain of computer vision use different techniques of AI to analyse the data provided to a computer program. There are many aspects involved in computer vision. For instance, in image processing, which is Subhasis's main interest, scientists focus on 2D images and how one image changes to another image in a video (essentially a series of photos). In pattern recognition, another field Subhasis works in, scientists instruct or program computers to use various methods to extract information from images using AI tools.

'Yes,' said Subhasis emphatically. He remembered the computer vision project that Professor Chatterjee had given him all those years ago, confident that he could solve the problem this time around.

This was in 1988. In the five years since Subhasis had worked on his thesis at IIT-KGP, computer systems had improved significantly. He had also gained more knowledge about how to design programs for computer vision applications. Subhasis figured that what the ophthalmologist needed was a computer program that was specially developed to scan photographs of patients' eyes to diagnose diabetic retinopathy. He began developing such a program.

What I need is a map of blood vessels of the retina, thought Subhasis. He read papers of scientists who were working on similar problems. Slowly, he developed the template of a healthy eye. The next step was to develop a computer program which would be able to detect patterns in photos of human eyes. If a photo had Pattern A, it would be considered healthy. If it had Pattern B, it could have diabetic retinopathy.

Once the code was done, Subhasis headed back to the eye doctor to test it. Much to the doctor's delight, the program was able to look at a photograph of the retina of patients and diagnose if they had diabetes!

In 1989, Subhasis and his colleagues published a scientific paper which included the template and the code they had written. It generated a lot of buzz among computer scientists the world over. Subhasis was happy

that his work would help doctors diagnose eye disorders more easily.

After completing his Ph.D, he moved back to India and joined IIT-B as an assistant professor in 1990. Once he settled in, he began looking for more challenging applications to work on in the field of computer vision.

One day, he entered his office and saw a stack of photos that someone had left on his desk. They were pictures from a conference he had attended. He noticed that in one of the photographs, there was someone standing behind him. The person's face was blurred. Subhasis could figure out that the person was standing a few metres behind him when the photo was taken.

'It's blurred. I can throw it away,' said his secretary.

I spy an inventor in this book who made a device to help doctors. What is the name of the device?

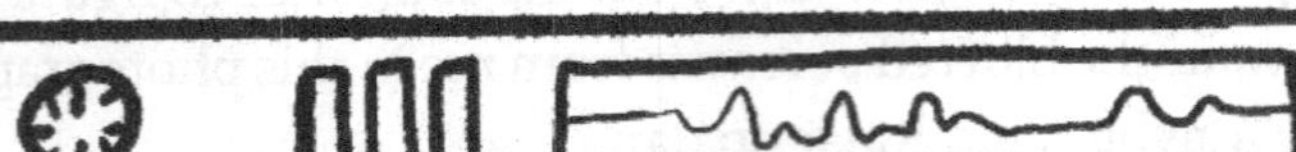

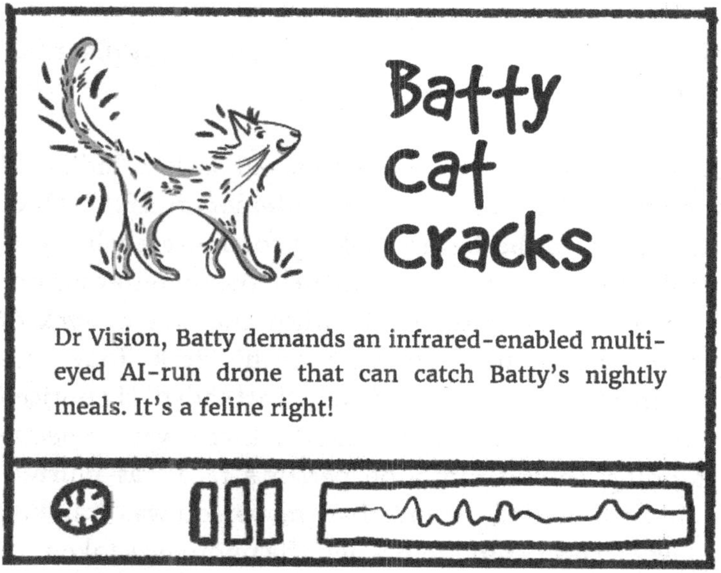

'Wait, wait, don't get rid of it just yet!' said Subhasis.

He had just found the next big problem he wanted to tackle in computer vision! Subhasis started reading up on what scientists were doing with blurred photographs using computer technology. He came across a problem called 'depth from defocus', which involved finding out how far a blurred object was from a sharper subject in a photo. It had been confounding computer vision scientists everywhere. He asked one of his students, AN Rajagopalan, to work with him on the project.

'Our eyes are unique because of our depth perception, which tells us how far away an object is from the other,' explained Subhasis. 'Can I ask the computer to figure out how far the blurred person is from me in this photograph?'

'Maybe,' said Rajagopalan.

Subhasis and Rajagopalan tried to apply the same solution that had worked for the diabetic retinopathy program. They tried comparing multiple images to see the difference between them. After a few months, the duo hit a dead end.

'It's not possible to compare two blurred images for depth,' said Subhasis. 'We have to try something else.' He continued to think about the problem all day in the hope of finding the solution.

Let me sleep on it, he thought. As soon as he lay down in bed, an idea struck him. He scrambled up and rushed to his study to note it down.

'There is another way to solve this,' Subhasis told Rajagopalan the next morning. 'We can look at how rays are bent by the lens.'

The reason photos were blurred, Subhasis deduced, was because the lens of the camera, depending on the lens setting, could focus the light coming from an object situated only at a particular distance away from the lens. Any object at that distance would appear sharp. Other objects, either too far or too near, would look blurred. Subhasis and Rajagopalan *taught* the computer to look at how far the lens was from the blurred object and how far it was from the sharper one.

To teach the computer to do this, they needed lots of blurred images. Soon, Subhasis and his students became famous on the IIT-B campus as the folks who collected blurred photographs! Finally, in 1998, Rajagopalan and Subhasis were able to finish coding and write a scientific paper on their research.

Subhasis wanted to develop this technology further. While thinking about it, he came across the concept of super-resolution. He knew that each photo was made up of pixels*. When you zoomed into photographs, they started to blur. Was there a way in which he could keep zooming into a photograph but still see the minute details that it had captured?

'If I can find a way to do that, it can help law enforcement agencies,' Subhasis said to himself. In the video footage from security cameras, the faces of the people captured were often blurred. This technology could help security agencies get a clearer image of the people recorded by the camera.

Subhasis enlisted his student Deepu Rajan to work with him. Together, they turned a sample video into a series of photographs. Each was slightly different from the other. They built a computer program to notice the difference in these photos.

'The computer program needs to find out changes between photographs, increase the size of the image, de-blur and reduce noise,' said Subhasis.

'That's a lot of things for a program to do!' exclaimed Deepu.

'If we do all of this together, we will have our super-resolution-making program,' said Subhasis.

It was a big task, but Subhasis relished tough problems. Building the computer program required

*A pixel is the smallest unit or building block of a digital image. Many pixels together form an image.

scanning through images and comparing them for minute differences. After two years of hard work, they were able to develop a program which could increase the resolution and make tiny image details more visible.

Using the findings from depth from blur and super resolution, Subhasis developed another unique computer program with which objects could be tracked in a video. This was especially useful for surveillance – the program could be run to automatically see thousands of videos.

The various technologies he created are being used in many applications. One of his programs is used by law enforcement and security agencies to scan a building and detect any cracks in the walls. 'It's like an X-ray of buildings,' explains Subhasis. Another company has used his technology to make a program which automatically flashes a 'Smoking is injurious to health' warning whenever there are smoking scenes in films.

Now as the director of IIT-B, Subhasis continues to push the frontiers of computer vision. He has been awarded the Shanti Swarup Bhatnagar Prize in recognition of his contributions.

But the biggest prize for Subhasis has been the satisfaction of solving big problems and helping people. 'Try to scientifically understand a tough problem and you will find the right solution,' he says. That includes making computers see like humans!

The Ultimate Science Crossword

ACROSS

4. A systematic study of materials and sources to establish facts and find new conclusions. (8)

6. A licence giving a sole right to a person to exclude others from making, using or selling an invention. (6)

7. A long essay involving personal research, written by a candidate for a university degree. (6)

DOWN

1. A person who has expert knowledge of one or more sciences. (9)

2. The top-most international prize for outstanding work in science. (5)

3. A magazine that deals with a particular scientific subject. (7)

5. Recorded observations, usually in numeric or textual form. (4)

7

A Camera for Subatomic Particles

It was a sunny day in the spring of 2009 in Geneva. It was a big day for Archana Sharma, and she was quite nervous. She sat outside the office of the Upgrade Committee, going over her presentation one last time.

Archana worked as a scientist at the Conseil Européen pour la Recherche Nucléaire, popularly known as CERN, the world's largest particle physics* laboratory. For six months now, she had been preparing to present a new idea to the other scientists for CERN's massive particle physics experiment: the Compact Muon Solenoid (CMS). The presentation mapped out Archana's dream; she wanted to create the largest gas electron multiplier (GEM) radiation detector† in the world.

*Particle physics is a branch of physics that studies subatomic levels of matter and radiation and interactions between them. These miniscule, invisible particles include electrons, protons and neutrons. Scientists also study very tiny particles produced by radiation, which are called photons, neutrinos and muons. See Page 102 for more details on particle physics.

†A gaseous detector is an instrument that uses a certain kind of gas to detect

She had the expertise. She was a global expert in gaseous detectors.

Even though the scientist, who had worked in the field of particle physics since 1989, was sure that she could do it, she was really anxious. Her visionary idea of developing giant GEM detectors had never been attempted before anywhere in the world (or perhaps the universe).

The CMS experiment involved 5,000 people, including particle physicists, engineers, technicians, students and support staff from over 200 institutes in 50 countries. It was one of the largest international scientific collaborations in the history of science! It consisted of a complex network of 70 million different information channels having to work together.

Since the CMS experiment was so big and so expensive, even a single wrong addition could crash the whole set-up. Archana's big dream was one with high stakes. Her project would cost millions of dollars to build. Scientists, technicians and experts from across the world had to collaborate. CERN's reputation was also on the line if her project failed.

It was like building a spaceship. You had to be very, very certain that each part you put in, be it a cord or a sensor, would work properly with the rest of the components, or your spacecraft would go kaput!

---

particles. When a charged particle passes through it, the instrument records and takes a photo of the invisible particle caused by high energy. This helps scientists study these particles and understand their behaviour. Archana specializes in creating different kinds of gaseous detectors.

To build her dream project, Archana had to convince *all* the other scientists and technicians who were working on the CMS experiment (that's 5,000 people!) that her idea was solid, and would help the experiment achieve breakthrough results.

The first step in the long chain of approvals that had to be sought was the Upgrade Committee. The door opened and she was called in. Archana shuffled through her papers, cleared her throat and told the Upgrade Committee about how she proposed to make the current small-sized GEM detectors bigger so that they could get more information out of the CMS experiment.

'But others have failed before to make this large-scale GEM detector, right?' asked one of the members of the committee.

'Yes,' Archana admitted.

'And this is an unproven technology,' stated another member. 'If you fail, the whole experiment will fail.'

'Yes,' replied Archana. 'But I won't fail.'

'This will not work for the CMS,' said a third person, shaking her head.

'It's too late to add a new technology into the CMS!' another person exclaimed.

Within 10 minutes, it was all over. Archana's idea had been rejected. She walked out disappointed, but she knew that rejection was the first step to success. 'There is a lot at stake. Of course they are hesitant. This will take time and patience. I need to prepare better,' Archana told herself. She had six months to get ready for the next meeting of the Upgrade Committee.

SCIENCE SPEAK

THE LARGEST LABORATORY MACHINE IN THE WORLD

What happens when you smash two things together? They break into smaller particles, of course. In 1954, a group of scientists from 12 countries in Western Europe came together with a single aim. They wanted to build an experiment where they could make particles of matter collide at ultra-high speeds to discover what they were made of. They were looking for answers, big and small. What were the subatomic particles that made up matter? How did the universe begin? What were the building blocks of life in the universe?

The team of scientists decided to make the world's largest particle smasher to

understand life itself. They were allotted an area on the border of France and Switzerland, near Geneva, to make their laboratory. This was the birth of CERN, a research facility that would operate the world's largest particle physics laboratory.

To discover what the basic particles of matter were, the particles had to be smashed really, really hard. They made particle accelerators in order to do this – special machines that use electromagnetic fields to make charged particles fly at extremely high speeds and crash into each other from opposite sides.

Over the next few decades, the scientists at CERN built the world's largest particle accelerators.

Today, there are more than 18,000 scientists from 110 countries working on various experiments at CERN. India too has joined CERN as an associate member and contributes 1.1% of the laboratory's annual budget. Like Archana, scientists from the various member countries have one goal: to find the secrets of the universe.

This time, she was determined to make the giant GEM detectors happen – she would find a way.

Archana had always possessed an uncanny knack for finding solutions to problems with innovative thinking. She first discovered this when she was in Class 11. One day, her physics teacher posed a question to the class. 'How do you reset a thermometer?' she asked.

'You can use a magnet,' Archana answered.

'How did you know that?' the teacher replied, surprised.

This concept had not been taught in class yet. Archana was surprised as well! She had not handled magnets and did not know *how* she knew that it could be used to reset a thermometer.

'You should become a physicist,' her teacher added.

After the class, Archana went to the library. She started exploring physics with growing fascination. That's when she discovered particle physics, and got hooked to it. Particle physics asked questions about the beginnings of life and its very nature. How did the universe form? How did we materialize? There were a lot of unsolved questions and Archana decided to use her gift for finding solutions in the world of physics.

After she graduated, Archana did a doctoral degree in nuclear physics (a branch of particle physics that investigates particles that make up radioactive matter). In 1987, she landed an incredible opportunity to visit CERN for three months. There she met Georges

Sleuth Snoop

I spy a sensor that is put on a spaceship to collect data from other planets. What is this machine called? Who is the scientist making it in one of the chapters?

____

____

Charpak, a Nobel Prize-winning French physicist who had developed gaseous particle detectors.

Meeting Charpak and interning at CERN opened her eyes to the possibilities of how big experiments in particle physics worked. She came to understand that one of the reasons Charpak could develop gaseous particle detectors was thanks to the infrastructure and experts available at CERN. She loved the idea of collaborating with people to work towards a common goal – to find answers to the impossible questions that had a humongous impact on our understanding of life.

'We can find the secrets of the universe through big experiments if we all work together,' she said to herself.

COLLIDERS. DETECTORS AND ELUSIVE PARTICLES

CERN has six particle accelerators. Of these, the biggest is the Large Hadron Collider (LHC). The machine lies in a tunnel that is 27 kilometres in circumference and is 175 metres deep under the CERN campus. It is the largest machine in the world!

In 2010, proton beams collided in the LHC and resulted in the release of a vast amount of energy and a swarm of subatomic particles. Thanks to the data from this collision, CERN scientists announced the discovery of a new subatomic particle named the Higgs-Boson in 2012.

This discovery was made because of another important type of tool called the detector. Installed along the 27-kilometre length of the LHC were eight information-collecting points called detectors. Their job was to take photos of the subatomic particles arising from the collision. The detectors were like millions of mobile phones stacked together inside the LHC, clicking pictures. Once they were taken, a multitude of scientists sifted through the photos to find undiscovered particles.

One of the important information-collecting points in the LHC is the Compact Muon Solenoid (CMS) experiment. The CMS explores if there are any other dimensions apart from the four dimensions we know of, and what dark matter is made of. The CMS itself consists of multiple detectors, is 21 metres long and weighs about 14,000 tonnes. That's equal to the weight of 7,000 male elephants!

Archana then returned to India and got married, and soon had a baby. But CERN remained on her mind. In 1989, the same laboratory at CERN offered her a post-doctoral position for three years. Her son was a year old and she had a lot of family commitments, but the opportunity was too good to refuse!

'I want to do this,' she told her family. And so, Archana moved to Geneva. She joined the research and development (R&D) department of the gaseous detector laboratory at the CMS experiment. The team was responsible for developing small-sized gaseous detectors, including the GEM detectors.

As the mother to an infant and a new joinee at CERN, the initial days were hard. Even though she had a strong academic background, she did not know how to do a lot of things, particularly when it came to working in the laboratory.

To know more about lab instruments, she did another Ph.D in instrumentation and learnt French. All this while taking care of a child on her own!

For 10 years, Archana brainstormed with 12 other scientists on developing more effective gaseous detectors at the R&D laboratory. She also became an expert on how to design, manufacture and test a gaseous detector.

In 2001, Archana was hired as a full-time CERN scientist. At that time, she was the only Indian scientist to become a staffer at the organization. This was truly a dream come true!

The week after her appointment, she was given her first big assignment as a full-time scientist. She was asked to build Resistive Plate Chambers (RPC) detectors, a type of gaseous detector. As an expert in the area, she would lead this project from scratch.

'You have to fill up an area of 1,000 square metres underground with two metre by one metre detectors,' she was told by the CERN committee.

Archana was astounded. That meant building enough detectors to cover a whole football field! Before this, she had only worked on small-sized detectors. The team gave her a key to a storehouse in the middle of CERN, which she could convert into her lab and workspace, and left.

It seemed too big a task. She went back home and cried, completely overwhelmed.

'You have to do this,' she told herself finally.

Squaring her shoulders, Archana built the laboratory she wanted. She got a piped gas system installed for mixing gas, flow meters to measure the flow of the gas, and components to make the RPC detectors, including frames, plates and electronics and computers to make simulations*. Alongside, she wrote documents detailing safety procedures and fire procedures, sanitation criteria, guidelines on how

*A simulation program is a software in which you model an experiment or a machine to see if it would operate the way it's meant to. Because machines today are really complex, scientists simulate the machine on their computers to see if all the parts will work together. Once they see it does, they develop a prototype, a physical example of the machine.

to handle equipment and processes to test each and every piece of equipment. With the laboratory ready for use, Archana and her team got down to building the first of the RPC detectors.

By 2004, the first detector was ready. The team was now made up of more than 20 scientists and students from different parts of the world: India, China, Pakistan, Korea, Italy and Germany. They began testing the detector by the stringent standards that had been set. As they were being tested, Archana's heart hammered. What if she failed? What if the detector did not work?

They tested the detectors one by one. The detectors whirred and kicked and showed the data as expected. The whole thing was tested again, just to be sure. 'It's working well,' said one of her students. Archana heaved a sigh of relief. The scientists celebrated that night!

'How are we going to take these detectors to the CMS project?' asked a student.

Archana was stumped. A simple thing like moving a part they were working on was going to be a challenge. Each detector weighed 200 kilograms and was made of delicate moving parts. The CMS experiment was 20 kilometres away from their laboratory and 100 metres underground. If they put the detector in a truck, it could damage the equipment, and all their hard work would go to waste. Archana designed a special trolley and a tool that could lift the detector and carry it to the entrance of the CMS experiment.

It was not over, though. Archana had to check if the detectors would work as part of the larger CMS experiment.

She went down to the site of the CMS experiment. The location was called Point 5. Archana and her team installed the RPC detectors in a side tunnel that led to the main LHC tunnel, and they worked! 'This is a big moment,' she told her teammates, urging them to get back to making more detectors.

By 2006, Archana's team had built 500 detectors and installed them underground. While building the RPC detectors, Archana had learnt how to do instrumentation, engineering, electronics, software simulations and data management.

As she continued to work at the underground facility of the CMS experiment, she noticed a gap. The RPC detectors covered a 1,000-square-metre area, the size of a football field. However, they could not take too much radiation heat. That's the reason why they were not installed close to the collision point in the main experiment. This led to an area of empty space in the innermost layer of the collision point, which had no detectors to record data and take pictures of the subatomic particles.

'What if I make big GEM detectors for this space?' Archana wondered aloud. She knew from experience that this type of detector could take the radiation heat close to the collision point. However, no one had ever tried to make large GEM detectors before.

FOXY FACTS

THE MOST POWERFUL COLLIDER IN THE WORLD

- The Large Hadron Collider, called LHC, is the most powerful particle smasher ever made by humans (we haven't checked with aliens yet!). If you go into the LHC with a thermometer, it will break. You see, the temperature in the underground tunnel is colder than outer space, a freezing -271.3° Celsius!
- CERN runs really, really expensive experiments. Its annual budget is 1.1 billion Euros.
- In April 2016, the LHC lost power because a small rodent chewed through its electrical wiring!

Over Christmas in 2008, the idea of building large detectors solidified in her mind. These GEM detectors would be placed in the empty space close to the CMS collision point. She was convinced that it would work. That's the reason she took her proposal to the Upgrade Committee.

'I want to design GEM detectors for the innermost layer of the CMS experiment,' she told the Upgrade Committee six months later. Her proposal was rejected again. Determined to make it work, Archana decided to make a prototype, a sample of the giant GEM detector. She talked to scientists who made GEM detectors in different parts of the world. Finally, she was able to convince a scientist in Belgium to collaborate with her. He assigned one of his students, Andre Marino, to work with her on the project.

In 2010, the world's most powerful particle accelerator, the LHC, began its first run. Five thousand scientists and engineers at CERN watched as the most powerful magnet on Earth was switched on for the first particle collision. The entire research facility burst into celebration.

Archana was busy working in her laboratory with two students building a large GEM detector.

In 2012, after many prototypes and failed experiments, Archana and her team were able to build a GEM detector which was one metre by a half square metre in dimensions. They switched it on, tested it and recorded the data.

'It's working,' whispered a thrilled Archana. No one had built a working prototype of such a big GEM detector before. This was the first of its kind in the world! With the prototype, Archana went to get the Upgrade Committee's approval again. *Third time's the charm*, she thought, as she presented. She was right. This time, it was approved!

Archana was ecstatic. She had passed the first hurdle. The next step was to get support from other institutions. Since it was an expensive project, she needed both grants and scientific expertise to help her out. She travelled around the world to speak to institutions in Germany, the USA and Italy to join her in developing giant GEM detectors.

She developed a technical proposal on how keeping detectors close to the collision point would improve the data collected from there. Armed with the proposal,

HORRIBLE HAIKU

Detector grabs
Scurrying particles
To perform a titanic
smash

Archana and her team, now consisting of 12 people, made a technical presentation to the CMS committee in 2013.

'The new GEM detectors will help sift through data collected in the experiment and help in finding new muons*,' said Archana to the technical committee.

Her technical proposal was approved. She spent the next year writing a detailed technical design report. The report illustrated its design, what materials would be used and how much it would cost. Archana submitted the report in December 2014, six years after the idea had first come to her. The project was going to cost $4.2 million.

Finally, in 2015, the project was approved for construction. She was able to raise $12.5 million for the GEM project. Archana moved to a new laboratory – a big 400-square metre space – to start developing the detectors. By then, the global GEM detector team had grown to include 300 scientists and experts from 40 institutions across 16 countries!

All of them came together to make Archana's giant GEM detectors! On 24 October 2019, they installed 144 detectors into the core of the CMS point.

*A muon is an elementary particle similar to the electron.

As you read this, Archana and her team are ramping up production. They are planning to make 288 more GEM detectors for 2023, and will develop and install 216 detectors in 2025. Archana has been looking forward to 2021, when the first particles will go through her giant GEM detectors.

Archana is proud of her achievement. However, she has a new dream – she wants to develop laboratories in India specializing in medical applications. 'I want to bring health technology from the laboratory to the people in India,' she says.

Draw the World's Biggest Invention

If you have a chance to make a massive invention like Archana, what will you make? Will it be a space carousel or a humongous forest?

Draw your giant invention and add in answers to these questions:

● What will it look like? ● What will it do? ● How will it work? ● What materials will you need to build it? ● How much will it cost? ● Who will use it and how? ● How will it be useful for living beings - humans, animals or plants?

8

Self-Growing Molecular Materials

It was the science teacher at Ayyappanpillai Ajayaghosh's school who showed him that chemistry was like magic. All you needed was a set of chemist's tools. Just like a witch made potions, you mixed different chemicals, and voila! You could create a new material or substance that came with magical possibilities.

That's the reason why Ajayaghosh decided in Class 10 that he would become a chemist, a scientist who specializes in the field of chemistry. It was not easy. His parents, who were farmers in a small village in Kerala, could barely afford his schooling. After he finished his graduation, he felt pressured to take up a job and support his family.

But Ajayaghosh had his heart set on becoming a chemist. He applied for a government fellowship offered by the Council of Scientific and Industrial Research (CSIR). This was in the 1980s, when the Indian government wanted to encourage scientists to invent

machines, medicines and products for the country. Chemistry was at the centre of all this scientific activity.

With the money he received from the fellowship, Ajayaghosh finished his doctoral studies and also managed to support his family. It was a tough life, but the young scientist loved it. In 1988, he joined the National Institute for Interdisciplinary Science and Technology (NIIST), a laboratory at CSIR. At the government-funded laboratory, he was free to do the research he wanted to do.

Once he had settled into his workplace, Ajayaghosh decided to build supramolecular nanomaterials* (see page 121). In the late 1980s, creating them was a challenging research area in chemistry.

Though the government was offering research grants to scientists, it was still expensive to work with nanomaterials. Ajayaghosh needed equipment like high-resolution microscopes, which were hard to find in India during the 1990s and were expensive to import. The chemist, however, kept himself motivated. He found scientists working with nanomaterials in international universities and collaborated with them. Later, he received grants from government funding agencies and slowly developed his laboratory, ordering the equipment he needed to do his research work from abroad.

*Nanomaterials are invisible materials that are very, very small. You cannot see them. Instruments and tools made with them are called nanodevices. Nanoscientists build these invisible machines and inject them, for instance, into the body for biosensing, bioimaging or diagnosing tumours. They can put nanomaterials in fabrics to make them stain-resistant. Nanomaterials can also be used to create air filters for viruses.

WHY SCIENCE NEEDS FUNDING

True discoveries and inventions take a while to shape up. To make them happen, scientists need to put in years of work. Scientific research also costs a lot of money. It needs expensive equipment like microscopes, genetic analysers, computers and servers. Most scientists, like Ajayaghosh, cannot afford to do science without financial funding, or grants, as scientists call them.

Scientists have different ways through which they receive these grants. Some are awarded by the government and some by wealthy patrons and private companies who want to promote science. Since the Government of India wants to encourage scientists to do research in cutting-edge fields, it sponsors a variety of grants. The Ministry of Science and Technology set up CSIR, which runs 38 laboratories across the country and funds 4,600 scientists. Ajayaghosh works in one such lab, the NIIST.

As Ajayaghosh set up his laboratory, he started to experiment and create superstructures made of molecules. He wanted to build a new nanomaterial by using a phenomenon called self-assembly, which involves putting a number of molecules together in a certain shape. After this, they start to communicate with each other electronically. Ajayaghosh wanted to understand if these molecules could also figure out what kind of building they wanted to be. Could he create a supramolecular structure that could build itself? Like an intelligent supramolecular structure!

'I want to find out how molecules talk to each other, and how their conversation can be converted to signals,' he told his students at the lab. These signals could then be used as sensors in the invisible devices that he wanted to build. It was a fascinating thought!

He decided to focus his research on a particular type of bond. 'Let us work with molecules that bond through pi systems,' he announced to his students. Pi systems are made of carbon molecules bonded together. These molecules are called fluorophores and are really sensitive. They blink or light up when a foreign molecule is around them. If Ajayaghosh could make nanomaterials using fluorophores and pi systems, they could have multiple applications, from sensing harmful disease molecules in the body to lighting up after a security breach in a digital system. They could even be used to create highly sensitive sensors to protect people from hazardous vapours like air pollution and viruses.

All Ajayaghosh had to do was build a stable supramolecular structure that could last. It took him months to develop a single nanomaterial. After it was made, he decided to test it thoroughly in his lab. 'We have to figure out if it will have a sufficient lifetime,' he told his team. The laboratory had special conditions to check how the material would function in different weather conditions. Were there any toxic elements in the material that could harm others? What was the reaction of the material to alkaline or acidic environments?

SCIENCE SPEAK

SPECTACULAR SUPRAMOLECULAR STRUCTURES

Everything, living or non-living, is made up of miniscule, invisible units called atoms or groups of atoms called molecules. A tree is made of molecules, as is water, air and every living being. But a tree is different from water, air or a cat, as each of them is made of different types of molecules. Simple molecules can connect to other molecules and form larger molecular complexes. In chemistry, this process is called bonding.

Chemists explore how molecules bond with each other in nature. They use this knowledge to make completely new substances in the laboratory called supramolecular structures. The process is similar to using bricks (which

are the molecules in this case) to build high-rise buildings (which are the supramolecular structures). A single supramolecular structure consists of billions or even trillions of molecules grouped together.

They are hard to create, needing a lot of patience and expensive equipment. These structures are also extremely small. A supramolecular structure can be anywhere between a nanometre and a micrometre, which is why they are also called nanomaterials. Ajayaghosh is the creator of many such nanomaterials.

Most of the nanomaterials they went on to create failed. Some were toxic, some decayed too quickly, and others were too expensive to reproduce industrially. 'We have to systematically evaluate all the reactions of these materials before they are market-ready,' said Ajayaghosh. For instance, if the material decayed because it was in the sun for too long, it could not be used in a currency note.

His high expectations made him difficult to work with. He pushed his students to perform and excel.

Batty cat cracks

Molecules bond with each other to make complex creatures like cats. Capisce, Batty buffs?

Some of them left midway, frustrated with the difficult nature of the work. Ajayaghosh, however, kept at it. One year became five. Five became 10, 15 and more. He developed hundreds of materials, tested them and then discarded them again and again. Every time he failed, he would start again, learning something that did not work. His single-minded aim was to create the perfect material.

In 1999, one of his students was working on a molecular problem when he found something unique. One of the molecules he was supposed to be working on was growing a little too quickly. Since Ajayaghosh had a reputation for being strict, he did not approach him immediately. Months later, when Ajayaghosh was talking to him, he saw some material that had gelled in a flask in one of the cupboards in the laboratory.

FOXY FACTS

A nanometre is a billionth part of a metre, completely invisible to the naked eye. The biggest (molecular) building that Ajayaghosh has made is just a few nanometres in size. A nanometre is tinier than the tiniest thing you can think of. Can you measure the things around you in nanometres?

- An ant is 50 lakh nanometres long.
- A sheet of paper is one lakh nanometres thick.
- A single hair on your head is one lakh nanometres wide.
- Your hand is about 10 crore nanometres long.
- Your fingernail grows at the rate of one nanometre per second. As you read this, they've grown two nanometres in length.
- A bacterium is about 1,000 nanometres long.

'What is that?' he enquired.

'Oh, the molecules you asked me to prepare,' replied the student nervously. 'I wanted to purify the molecules, but when I was dissolving them, this happened.'

Ajayaghosh stared at it. The material had expanded, like a forest in the bottle. It was a soft, bulky material and it emitted light. When they tried putting solvent on it, it became both soft and solid. 'This is amazing!' whispered Ajayaghosh. 'This has turned into a gel. Why didn't you show it to me before?'

The student mumbled something sheepishly in response. On closer inspection, Ajayaghosh realized that they had found a new property of the pi system, something that had not been discovered so far.

The nanomaterial was soft, malleable and could be shaped into nanodevices, offering many possibilities. Ajayaghosh was excited! Along with his students, he started exploring its nature and properties. The team named these materials π-gels (pi-gels).

The first step was to control the nanomaterial's growth. They worked on it for months, reshaping it and introducing new molecules and bonds to see how it would behave. After a lot of trial and error, they were able to insert new elements into the pi-gel that controlled its size and shape.

Next, the team experimented on putting the nanomaterial through stress. To do this, Ajayaghosh poured alkaline liquids and acid on it, put it through various temperatures and measured its properties under X-ray. He tested how the material would age, hit it

Sleuth Snoop

I spy a scientist who builds nanosensors. Can you name them and the chapter they are in?

with a nanohammer and even put weights on it, trying to see how durable it was in different environments.

As a fundamental scientist, Ajayaghosh was interested in basic science and not in practical inventions (See the difference between basic and applied science on Page 143). In 2001, he created a nanomaterial that was truly magical! He had made a π-gel that could build itself. In scientific terms, this meant that the nanomaterial could self-assemble. Meanwhile, the architect, Ajayaghosh, could just sit back and have a cup of tea.

This step was quite crucial as the self-assembled nanomaterials could now be used as a building or a scaffolding to control electronic energy or light. These gel-like materials could be used for anything from energy conservation and optical sensors to bomb

detectors. They could be used to make cheap solar cells, biodegradable electronics or even 3D printed electronics. The possibilities were endless!

It was the miracle material that Ajayaghosh had imagined when he had first started working as a scientist. It had taken him 20 years, but he finally did create the nanomaterial that he had dreamed of. Ajayaghosh received several awards, including the Shanti Swarup Bhatnagar Prize for Chemical Sciences, the Infosys Science Prize and The World Academy of Science (TWAS) chemistry prize.

Currently, a start-up has begun creating products using Ajayaghosh's π-gels. Now the director at CSIR-NIIST, the passionate chemist has kick-started work on nanomaterials that can protect currency and valuable documents. 'Chemistry is exciting. Without molecules, there is no life, no materials, no fun,' he says.

SCIENCE SPEAK

WHY IS CHEMISTRY SUCH A COOL, BIG DEAL?

Chemists like Ajayaghosh create new substances. Other than nanomaterials, chemists have created plastics, medicines, fibres like nylon, and other substances that are used in everyday life. List 10 materials that you think were created by chemists. We will start you off!

1 Plastic bucket ______

2 ______

3 ______

4 ______

5 ______

6 ______

7 ______

8 ______

9 ______

10 ______

Colour Me Chemical

What do you see in a chemistry laboratory? Can you write down the names of the equipment pictured here? After you are done, colour them in.

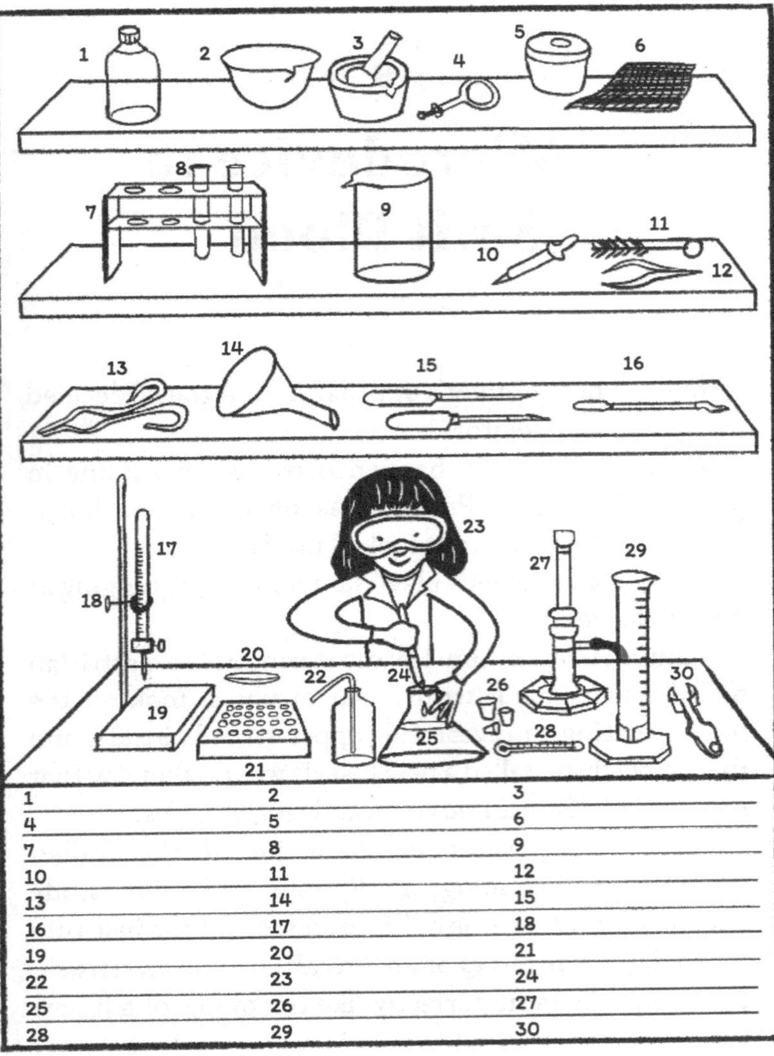

1	2	3
4	5	6
7	8	9
10	11	12
13	14	15
16	17	18
19	20	21
22	23	24
25	26	27
28	29	30

9

A Microdevice to Split Blood

It was on a hot summer's day that Amit Agrawal decided to become an inventor.

An electrician had happened to visit his home in Allahabad in Uttar Pradesh. As he repaired a burnt socket, 10-year-old Amit looked on, fascinated.

'Amit, come on, let's play!' said his cousin, tugging at Amit's sleeve.

Amit didn't hear him. He was staring as the electrician pulled a wire, cut it with a pair of pliers, took off the plastic coating to reveal the copper strands inside, and then expertly installed a new fuse. It was on that day that Amit decided he wanted to fix and create things.

After finishing school, Amit joined the Indian Institute of Technology in Kanpur (IIT-K) to study engineering. When one of his professors at the institute showed him the pump of an aircraft, he was awestruck. The components fit perfectly like the pieces of a jigsaw

puzzle – the piston, cylinders, drainage and pumps were all compactly put in.

'Everything is so efficient!' exclaimed Amit. 'It's beautiful.'

Amit wanted to build machines that were designed to be efficient. When he was done with college, he joined Tata Motors in Pune as an engineer. As part of the maintenance team, his job was to ensure that the machines in the automobile factory (some as big as half a room!) worked well. The machines were used to manufacture car parts, like the outer shell and the engine. Amit loved working with machines and tinkering with them to make sure that they were well-maintained. Happy machines on the assembly line meant that they could manufacture good-quality cars!

Though he liked his job, Amit kept going back to his original dream – to be an inventor of efficient machines. After a few years at his job, he decided to study further. He did a Ph.D in experimental fluid mechanics* in the USA.

In 2003, he began working on microdevices, small coin-sized machines which were used in electronics. He discovered them when he was doing his postdoctoral work.

Everything from computers and mobile phones to televisions needed them, and there were only a few laboratories around the world that were building them.

*Experimental fluid mechanics is a branch of physics that researches fluids and how they flow.

Find the other scientist in this book who also works in fluid mechanics.

____

Amit also figured out something unique about microdevices. They were relatively cheap to make and could be used in remote areas. This technology could really benefit a country like India, with its vast population and limited resources.

In 2004, Amit became a professor in the department of mechanical engineering at IIT-B. As soon as he was assigned a laboratory, he started working on the designs of the microdevices that he intended to make. The first step was to find out what kind of invention would be useful to people.

That's when he came across the concept of microchannels. Since microdevices were small machines, it was hard to build channels, or micro-sized lines, on them, through which water could flow.

HOW TO BECOME AN INVENTOR

You don't need to study a lot to invent something. All you need is a problem and a creative solution. Check out these early inventors who have made waves in our country recently!

- Kavya Vignesh, 12, built a Bee Saver Bot. This device could relocate a beehive in her neighbourhood.
- Arman Gupta, 10, hated cleaning his room. He built a remote-controlled cleaning robot to do it for him.
- In a village in Haryana, Avneet, 13, designed a solar bike to travel to his school, which was 20 kilometres away.
- Remya Jose, 14, invented a low-cost washing-cum-exercise machine. You had to cycle to produce electricity to make the machine work.

Follow these steps to invent something.

Find a problem to solve: Observe your home, school and neighbourhood. Is there a problem that needs to be solved? Jot down a possible solution in your notebook.

Make sure your idea doesn't already exist: Do a search online to see if something similar has already been done.

Sketch your idea: Draw out a basic diagram of your invention. What will it look like? What material will you use to build it?

Build the prototype: Make a working sample of your invention.

Test your prototype: Does the machine do what you thought it would? Ask your friends and family to use it. Does it solve the problem you set out to work on?

Reach out to investors: Once your prototype is ready, find businesses who want to produce and sell it in the market.

Though they were tough to create, microchannels had plenty of uses in microdevices. The simplest, and the most important one, was in microchips, which powered laptops and phones. The chips of an electronic device generated heat and needed to be cooled down. If Amit could make tiny microchannels and flow water through them, they could be used in future chip designs to cool smartphones.

As Amit had a doctorate in fluid mechanics, he used his knowledge to build the channels. He asked a few of his students to work with him on the project.

Making a small passage was easy. All you had to do was etch or scratch the surface of a microdevice, which was made of a type of plastic. But what was difficult was closing the passage and controlling a fluid's flow.

'Water should flow through the passage and not around it or beyond it,' said Amit, after a failed experiment, to one of his students, Shiv Govind Singh. They had been working on the problem to control the flow in the microchannel for months now and had been failing.

One day, Shiv was working on the microchannel, when he found a new substance – a glue or paste that could plug the channel and stop the water from leaking. He hurried to Amit's room and showed him the microchannel that he had used the glue on. Amit was stunned. He checked the channel, and checked it again. They found out that the microchannel could indeed control water flow. This was a big achievement! It also meant that Amit could now start building the efficient microdevices he had envisioned.

Shiv left the lab to study further, and Amit continued to work on his passion project. He thought about what kind of microdevice he could design with the microchannels.

'Could we flow blood in there and help doctors?' suggested a student.

Amit thought about it. It would be difficult to accomplish, but it had been his dream to create devices that would help humanity. He agreed, and they began their research on what kind of device would be useful to doctors and patients. Since they were not from a medical background, Amit and his students went to a nearby hospital to understand what problems doctors faced the most. How could microdevices help them? It was during one of these discussions that Amit found that most doctors faced a problem that had to do with blood testing.

If a doctor wanted to know if a patient had dengue, they'd take a blood sample. This sample would then be sent to the pathology laboratory. There, a technician used two machines to test the blood. The first machine, the centrifuge, spun the blood at high speeds in order to break it down. Plasma*, the gooey yellow part of the blood, was then extracted and sent for diagnosis. The second machine tested the plasma to check for any infection. Finally, the technician would make a report and send it back to the doctor. Only then could the doctor tell if the patient had an infection. Diagnosis could take anything from two days to a week.

*Plasma is the largest part of our blood – about 55 per cent of it. It has an important role – it ferries nutrients, salts and enzymes throughout the body.

Batty cat cracks

Dr Inventor, can you create a separator to scout a mouse in a garbage bin? You shall have Batty's eternal gratitude. *Meowr.*

'We can reduce the time that doctors wait for laboratory reports!' exclaimed Amit. He had an idea, a simple one. He wanted to make a microcentrifuge to break down blood into plasma instantly. There would be no need to send the blood sample to a lab for testing!

He read through entire libraries and did a ton of online research to find out if such a device existed anywhere in the world. There was nothing like it.

He decided to go ahead and create the microcentrifuge, calling it a blood-plasma separation microdevice. Amit and his students drew out a model on the computer. The prototype took shape slowly, with collective thinking and many changes to the design. There were challenges, of course. Though Amit had successfully used water in microchannels, blood was thicker than water. They had to redesign the microchannels.

The second challenge was to find real blood. They went to pathology labs and blood banks, but were met with suspicious questions. Even though they needed just five millilitres of blood – as much as a sip of water – they needed to keep it fresh to test it on their prototype. Soon, Amit gained a reputation on campus.

'This professor likes blood,' whispered one student.

'You mean like a vampire?' said another, laughing.

For a year they tried but failed to make a working prototype. It seemed like an endless cycle – design, make a prototype and then test it. Fail, go back and design, make a prototype and then test it again. Then one day, one of Amit's students, Siddharth Tripathi, asked him to get to the lab immediately.

'Sir, there is something yellow coming out of the device,' he reported, excitedly.

Amit observed the microdevice. Sure enough, a yellow fluid oozed out of the machine. 'This is plasma!' he exclaimed. Finally, the microdevice had been able to successfully separate the plasma from human blood.

In 2011, Amit had made his first working prototype. It was a simple version, but it worked.

During the demonstration, he found more ways to improve on the current design. He decided to change the layout of the blood flow and the dimensions to increase efficiency. His mind was already visualizing a better, second-generation version of the plasma separator that could separate plasma from blood more efficiently.

After two years, he had a new and improved version ready. However, Amit was not yet satisfied. The

microdevice didn't seem efficient enough. He got back to the laboratory and changed the geometry of the flow passage, the dimensions and the flow rate.

In 2015 – five years after he had begun work on the microcentrifuge – Amit designed something that worked efficiently and beautifully, just like the aircraft pump he had been inspired by many years ago. The third-generation plasma separator worked brilliantly. The device could separate 100 per cent of the plasma from blood samples, and took very little time to do it. Amit filed for patents for his separator.

As of today, the plasma separator has been licensed to a start-up in Pune that works on building microdevices in the healthcare sector. So the next time you go to the doctor with an infection, they might just use Amit's blood-plasma separator to test your blood!

Meanwhile, Amit and his students have already moved on to their next invention. They are developing a microdevice that can detect cancer in the early stages. 'I love designing different functionalities in a device, changing it and tweaking it to get a result,' he explains, adding that being an inventor is the best way to live.

HORRIBLE HAIKU

A mechanical
molecule
Scurries through
tiny channels
Peeking out of
smartchips

Which Simple Machines Do I Use?

Machines are used by all of us in our everyday lives. Below are six types of simple machines. First, match the machines with their descriptions. Second, match the description to the image of the appliance at your home.

1. INCLINED PLANE	**A.** A rod that tilts on a pivot to produce a useful action at another point.	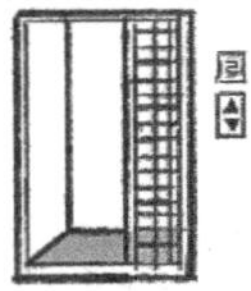
2. WHEEL AND AXLE	**B.** A sloping surface, it reduces the effort needed to raise loads.	
3. PULLEY	**C.** A shaft with a thread or a groove. The screw holds things together by turning and moving into surrounding material.	
4. LEVER	**D.** A device that turns around a fixed point to act as a rotating lever.	
5. WEDGE	**E.** A grooved wheel that turns on an axle over which a rope, chain or belt passes. The groove fixes the rope or cable so that it won't slip off.	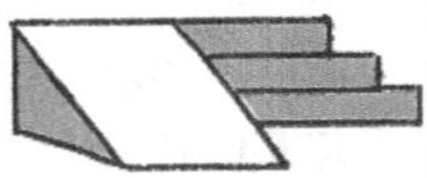
6. SCREW	**F.** A part of a machine with a sloping side that moves to exert force.	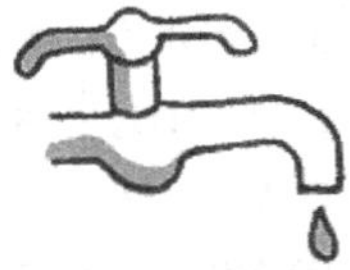

10

Electricity in Invisible Tubes

One day, in high school, Ajay Sood's science teacher was teaching the class about Bernoulli's principle. 'The principle states that an increase in the speed of a fluid occurs when there is either a decrease in static pressure or in the fluid's potential energy,' said the teacher.

'Ma'am,' asked Ajay, 'does physics have an answer to everything?'

'Yes, of course,' said his teacher. 'If you apply the scientific method.'

Ajay learnt that physics was the oldest form of science. With its concepts, you could find answers to all things, big and small. You could understand the great mysteries of the universe as well as the secrets of tiny, invisible atoms. As he cycled back home from school (a distance of 12 kilometres – in Jalandhar, Punjab), his teacher's words rang in his head. Physics could tell him how electricity worked, how a fan moved and why his cycle went faster when he pedalled

harder. It could also give him the answers to why the Earth rotated around the sun and how the universe was formed.

As soon as he reached home, he ran to the living room where his parents sat and said, 'I want to understand how everything works. I want to study physics!'

'You will need to work very hard and for many years,' his mother replied.

Ajay nodded. To find the answers to phenomena grand and mundane, from the workings of the universe to the mechanics of his cycle, he was ready to work hard.

Ajay did a postgraduate course in physics at the Punjab University, followed by a Ph.D in physics at IISc in Bengluru. In 1973, he began working as a physicist at the Indira Gandhi Centre for Atomic Research at Kalpakkam in Tamil Nadu. There he specialized in researching condensed matter physics*.

One day, while he was taking a dip with his friends at the Kalpakkam beach, a huge wave pulled him in. He panicked, swimming hard.

He came out, his heart beating, his mind whirring. 'Water!' he gasped.

His friends offered him a sip of water.

'No,' he said. 'Water molecules! We need to dive deeper into them.'

His friends frowned, confused. They hoped Ajay had not hit his head too hard. Ajay dried himself, headed back

*Condensed matter physics is a type of physics in which a scientist studies the complex relation between many particles. They could study how different types of solids interact with liquids, gases, plasmas, etc.

to his office and steered his research in a new direction. He wanted to understand how water molecules behaved at the nanolevel. His near-death experience had given him an idea. It was an intriguing question about basic science that would consume him for years to come.

In 1988, Ajay joined IISc, where he took up nanoscience, the study of tiny objects, about one to two thousand times smaller than the thickness of human hair. He wanted to understand how atoms, the building blocks of the material world, acted with each other on the nano scale.

He was especially curious to explore a nanomaterial created by a Japanese physicist in 1991. Called a carbon nanotube (CNT), it was made of carbon atoms, a hundred thousand times thinner than a single strand of human hair. Since the tube was so tiny and thin, Ajay felt that it could become a channel or a direction for electrons to move in.

Ajay wondered if a liquid or gas could move through this carbon nanotube and produce electricity. That would mean producing an electric current without a battery! He built an experiment in his laboratory, along with one of his students, Shankar Ghosh. They wanted to observe if the movement of water molecules through nanotubes could drag electrons* and create an electric current.

*Electrons are subatomic particles, part of an atom, that carry an electric charge and generate electric current when they move.

SCIENCE SPEAK

ARE YOU A BASIC OR APPLIED SCIENTIST?

Some scientists study problems that don't seem to have much of an impact on our daily lives. For example, biologists who catalogue every type of plant and animal in the rainforest, or mathematicians who do theorems or physicists who ask questions about what stars are made of.

These types of scientists work in what is called basic science. The goal of basic science is to understand how things work. How did the universe begin? What is a cell made of? What are protons, neutrons and electrons composed of?

Scientists like Ajay Sood, who work in basic science, are driven by curiosity or interest in a scientific question. They apply scientific methods to this question to find out if the hypothesis they have made is correct.

Applied science, on the other hand, applies discoveries to new technologies. Applied scientists create machines, medicines, spacecraft and computers that are of immediate value to the world.

If you design a windmill, you are an applied scientist. If you find out how wind makes energy, you are working in basic science. We need both to create a better world.

Write down three science questions you can solve in applied and basic science.

Applied Science

Can I make a lens for the blind to help them see?

____

____

____

Basic Science

What makes my eyes see?

____

____

____

They ran experiments for a few months. Late one night, Ajay was sitting in the lab along with Shankar, when something unexpected happened. The water molecules moved through the nanotube, producing a tiny amount of current, or electricity. They were thrilled! They had discovered a new property of nanotubes – the flow of liquids and gases through single-walled carbon nanotubes could create electrical energy. The two physicists published their results and the discovery was talked about by scientists around the world. The effect came to be known as the Sood effect, named after Ajay.

There were many uses for the Sood effect. Using this discovery, inventors could create self-powered

pacemakers[*] that could work on human blood as batteries and track the heart's health. Ajay and his student patented the discovery, but they didn't stop there.

'Let's try flowing gas through the nanotube now,' exclaimed Ajay. Flowing gas through nanotubes also produced electricity, telling them that their initial hypothesis was right. But something was off.

'Sir, the voltage[†] produced is not proportional to the velocity[§],' frowned Shankar.

'That's impossible,' replied Ajay.

Both of them did the experiment again. The experiment had worked, proving their initial hypothesis, but something new had been revealed. The results made Ajay wonder if their understanding of the reason why the electric current was created was correct in the first place. The voltage generated through gas seemed to behave differently than water.

'This is fascinating,' said Ajay. For days, he could not sleep well as the experiment had left him perplexed. Late one night, an idea struck him. He hurriedly dressed up and cycled to his laboratory, heading to his office to pick up one of his old college textbooks. He read

*A pacemaker is a small device that is placed in the chest to track or control heart rhythms.

†Voltage is the pressure exerted by a power source that pushes charged electrons or electric current through a conducting loop, enabling the current to do work like lighting up a bulb. Voltage is measured in volts.

§Velocity is the direction of the movement of the body or the object or the distance covered by it in a unit of time.

something, almost dropped the book in his excitement and promptly called Shankar. 'Shankar, come now! It's simple, basic physics!'

The reason gas had behaved differently was because of Bernoulli's principle, something that Ajay had learnt in high school. 'There are different pressures along the flow that give rise to temperature differences,' said Ajay. It was this phenomenon that led to the electric signal that the gas generated. Ajay was excited about it as it could be used to create sensors that could potentially track gas flow in car engines or gas pipes. This discovery could also be used in energy-saving devices. Ajay and Shankar patented their idea, and a company in the USA licensed this patent to develop a product.

Being a basic scientist, Ajay had limited interest in working on the applications of his invention, though. He has moved on to other research work since then. 'Applications are important,' he says. 'But I'm more interested in finding the answers to difficult questions.'

For his extraordinary work in nanotechnology, Ajay has received the Bhatnagar Award, the GD Birla Award and the Third World Academy of Sciences Prize. All these trophies lie on a shelf in his home, gathering dust. The physicist and professor is more excited by the problems that he wants to solve.

Currently, Ajay is working on something called flocking, which explains the physics of how groups of people or objects behave when they are together.

Batty cat cracks

Dr Physics, do you know that Batty's heart turns into electric goo every time she sees a mouse hopping in a corner?

How do humans move in a group? Is there an explanation in physics for it? Again, the principles he has found could benefit society at large. He is hoping that applied scientists pick up his research and use it to create useful technology that improves life.

Ajay's love of physics keeps him working in the laboratory for up to 10 hours every day. 'Curiosity and physics will give you an answer to everything,' he says, 'from how a machine works to how a planet moves.' Nothing can remain a mystery if you are a physicist!

SCIENCE SPEAK

HOW TO BECOME A SCIENTIST

A scientific method is a process of experimentation that is used to explore the universe and the world around us. This is the method used by scientists everywhere. Here's how you can become one!

1. **Ask a question:** The first step to inventing or discovering something is to ask a question. What makes a fan move when you switch it on?
2. **Do background research:** Once you have a question, find out if someone else already knows the answer to it by doing an online search or reading books in the library.
3. **Construct a hypothesis:** You have a question that has not been answered by anyone, anywhere in the world? Perfect.